B

D0044939

STAR WARS

FASCINATING FACTS

STORY, LORE & HISTORY FROM THE
GREATEST GALAXY

PABLO HIDALGO

**PORTABLE
PRESS**
San Diego, California

Portable Press
An imprint of Printers Row Publishing Group
10350 Barnes Canyon Road, Suite 100, San Diego, CA 92121
www.portablepress.com • mail@portablepress.com

Copyright © 2020 Lucasfilm Ltd.

All rights reserved. No part of this publication may be reproduced, distributed, or transmitted in any form or by any means, including photocopying, recording, or other electronic or mechanical methods, without the prior written permission of the publisher, except in the case of brief quotations embodied in critical reviews and certain other noncommercial uses permitted by copyright law.

Printers Row Publishing Group is a division of Readerlink Distribution Services, LLC. Portable Press is a registered trademark of Readerlink Distribution Services, LLC.

Correspondence regarding the content of this book should be sent to Portable Press, Editorial Department, at the above address.

Publisher: Peter Norton • Associate Publisher: Ana Parker
Senior Developmental Editor: April Graham Farr
Developmental Editor: Diane Cain
Editor: Jessica Matteson
Production Team: Jonathan Lopes, Rusty von Dyl, Beno Chan

Author: Pablo Hidalgo
Cover and Interior Designer: John J. Hill
Interior Designer: Keith Plechaty

ISBN: 978-1-68412-895-2

Printed in China

24 23 22 21 20   1 2 3 4 5

INTRODUCTION

Star Wars is a deep well. It's a galaxy brimming with interesting characters and fascinating history, as well as a film series full of ingenious innovation and talented artists. Its appeal has so many layers— which is partly why it continues to find success after more than forty years—and draws in audiences from all ages. As newcomers to the saga peel away layers of story, lore, and history and discover far more underneath, *Star Wars* grows with them, rewarding deeper exploration.

This book is a portable portal to that well of information. The facts found within are not an exhaustive chronicle of the saga or its making. Instead, they are select bits of information drawn from across all nine films of the Skywalker Saga, meant to delight and

astonish. Some can be classified as lore, information gleaned from the universe as described in the stories. Some are more grounded, based on our planet and our history of enjoying *Star Wars* as an entertainment juggernaut. An index in the back will help you navigate the topics covered. It stretches back to the early 1970s, when *Star Wars* was just a germ of an idea in George Lucas's head, all the way to 2019's epic finale of the saga, *Star Wars: The Rise of Skywalker*.

Whether it's browsing through these pages for an eyebrow-raising anecdote to impress your *Star Wars* pals or seeking out a suitable mic-drop moment for a *Star Wars* trivia competition, this book has you covered with its hundreds of fascinating facts.

A *STAR WARS* IS BORN

On August 3, 1971, United Artists registered the title "The Star Wars" with the Motion Picture Association of America, as part of a two-picture deal it signed with filmmaker George Lucas. The first picture, *American Graffiti* (released in 1973), was destined to become Lucas's first smash hit. The second picture was just hazily defined as a "space fantasy adventure in the vein of *Flash Gordon*," which the studio eventually passed on. Their loss would prove to be 20th Century Fox's eventual win.

THE SECRET EWOKESE
INGREDIENT

To craft convincing-sounding *Star Wars* languages, sound designer Ben Burtt would turn to exotic tongues from our planet as a starting point. The Jawa language started with Swahili, for example; Huttese finds its roots in Quechuan, an indigineous Peruvian language. For Ewokese, Burtt was drawn to the cadence and words of Kalmyk Oirat, a Mongolian language. He found an 80-year-old speaker willing to speak at length on tape, provided she had her preferred beverage on hand. This penchant caused her to be nicknamed "Grandma Vodka."

GOT IT
WHERE IT COUNTS

Technical Name:
Corellian Engineering
Corporation YT-1300f
modified light freighter

You Know it As:
Millennium Falcon

Size Specs:
34.4 meters long,
25.6 meters tall

Performance:
Sublight speed of 75 MGLT*;
atmospheric speed of
1,050 kph

Weaponry:
• Two CEC AG-2G
quad laser turrets
• Two Arakyd concussion
missile tubes
• AX-108 "Ground buzzer"
blaster cannon

Key Features:
• Tricked-out navicomputer
and modified engines
• Military-grade armor plate
• Sensor-proof smuggling
compartments

* MGLT is a standardized unit of sublight
speeds that take into account varying
interstellar conditions.

The *Millennium Falcon* is far more than a simple light freighter. Under the stewardship of dapper Lando Calrissian, the *Falcon* was a sleek sportsman's ship, with smooth lines and hidden features, like a secondary launch vehicle/escape pod. Under Han Solo's care (or lack of it), the *Falcon* became the galaxy's fastest hunk of junk, its dilapidated exterior and unpredictable subsystems leading many—by design—to underestimate its performance. Solo lost track of the ship after settling down to become a family man, but when his life was upended by the loss of his son to the dark side, he made it his mission to track it down again.

HIGH-FLYING COSPLAY

In conjunction with the latest *Star Wars* films, ANA—the largest airline in Japan—dressed up jets in their fleets as *Star Wars* droids. This includes an R2-D2 jet (a B787-9), a BB-8 jet (a B777-300), and a C-3PO jet (a B777-200). Anthony Daniels actually signed the C-3PO one when it was unveiled at the Tokyo/Haneda airport in a special ceremony.

THE ONE AND ONLY
LANDO CALRISSIAN

Leigh Brackett's first draft of *Empire*'s screenplay has an unusual backstory for the charming rogue Lando Calrissian. "I'm a clone. Of the Ashardi family," he says. "My great-grandfather wanted many sons and he produced them from the cells of his own body. His sister, a remarkable woman, produced many daughters by the same means. Thus we keep the blood pure." This fact did not appear in any subsequent drafts, and the thread was completely abandoned, thus keeping Lando forever one-of-a-kind.

TWO-INCH LIFTS

Rob Inch served as stunt supervisor on *The Force Awakens* and *The Last Jedi*, offering some saga continuity and lightsaber expertise thanks to his particularly unique experience. He fought in the prime of the Jedi, after all, as he was Liam Neeson's stunt double in *The Phantom Menace*, picking up a lightsaber to do battle with the evil Darth Maul. "Liam is really tall," Inch said. "I think he's six-foot-four-inches. So I still had to wear two-inch lifts to double for him!"

LUKE SKYWALKER'S TIMELINE

Born on Polis Massa along with twin sister Leia to Padmé Amidala; taken by Obi-Wan Kenobi to the Lars homestead on Tatooine

Age 19: After the Empire torches the homestead in the search for rebel droids, Luke apprentices himself to Obi-Wan Kenobi.

Age 19: As an X-wing pilot, destroys the Death Star by trusting in the Force and making a one-in-a-million shot.

Age 22: Now a commander in the Rebel Alliance, Luke leads the defense of Echo Base on Hoth against Imperial attack.

Age 22: Luke interrupts his training with Jedi Master Yoda to face Vader and learns Vader is his father.

Age 23: Luke surrenders to the Empire and is taken before Emperor Palpatine, where he faces the temptation of the dark side.

Age 23: After saving his father from the dark side, Luke begins training his sister in the ways of the Force.

Age 34: Luke begins instructing his nephew, Ben Solo, in the Force.

Age 50: A disastrous misunderstanding between Luke and his nephew results in the destruction of his Jedi Order, the creation of Kylo Ren, and Luke's fleeing into exile.

Age 53: In one last act of Jedi heroism and Force mastery, Luke saves the Resistance and becomes one with the Force.

Age 54: Luke's spectral form advises Rey as she faces the Sith Eternal uprising on Exegol.

STORMTROOPER
HITS KEEP COMING

Nigel Godrich, a hit record producer from England, is best known for producing all of Radiohead's albums. As a *Star Wars* fan, he has the distinction of being killed twice on-screen as a First Order stormtrooper. In *The Force Awakens*, he plays FN-9330, stationed at Starkiller Base when he has the bad luck to run into an armed Chewbacca, who sends him reeling with a blast from a Wookiee bowcaster. In *The Rise of Skywalker*, Godrich played FN-2808, a stormtrooper on Pasaana who gets an arrow in the visor courtesy of a disguised Lando Calrissian. "I'm sort of working my way through the entire cast," joked Godrich. "Maybe everyone can have a go."

WHEN IT RAINS...

During the first week of location shooting on *Star Wars*, Tunisia was hit with its first winter rainstorm in 50 years, cutting the March 26, 1976, shoot early and forcing a weekend of production so as not to fall behind schedule. Among the scenes requiring reshuffling was Luke looking out onto the Tatooine sunset.

THE CANTINA SHOWDOWN
STAR WARS: A NEW HOPE

INT. TATOOINE - MOS EISLEY - CANTINA
Luke is terrified but tries not to show it. He quietly
sips his drink, looking over the crowd for a more
sympathetic ear or whatever. A large, multiple-eyed
Creature gives Luke a rough shove.

> CREATURE
> Negola dewaghi wooldugger?!?

The hideous freak is obviously drunk. Luke tries to
ignore the creature and turns back on his drink. A
short, grubby Human and an even smaller rodent-like
beast join the belligerent monstrosity.

> HUMAN
> He doesn't like you.

> LUKE
> I'm sorry.

> HUMAN
> I don't like you either.

The big creature is getting agitated and yells some
unintelligible gibberish at the now rather nervous,
young adventurer.

> HUMAN (continuing)
> Don't insult us. You just watch yourself.
> We're wanted men. I have the death sentence
> on twelve systems.

> LUKE
> I'll be careful then.

                    HUMAN
                You'll be dead.

The rodent lets out a loud grunt and everything at
the bar moves away. Luke tries to remain cool but
it isn't easy. His three adversaries ready their
weapons. Old Ben moves in behind Luke.

                     BEN
        This little one isn't worth the effort.
            Come let me buy you something.

A powerful blow from the unpleasant creature sends
the young would-be Jedi sailing across the room,
crashing through tables and breaking a large jug
filled with a foul-looking liquid. With a blood-
curdling shriek, the monster draws a wicked chrome
laser pistol from his belt and levels it at old Ben.
The bartender panics.

                  BARTENDER
           No blasters! No blasters!

With astounding agility old Ben's laser sword sparks
to life and in a flash an arm lies on the floor. The
rodent is cut in two and the giant multiple-eyed
creature lies doubled, cut from chin to groin. Ben
carefully and precisely turns off his laser sword and
replaces it on his utility belt. Luke, shaking and
totally amazed at the old man's abilities, attempts
to stand. The entire fight has lasted only a matter of
seconds. The cantina goes back to normal, although
Ben is given a respectable amount of room at the bar.
Luke, rubbing his bruised head, approaches the old
man with new awe.

―――――――――

A version of this cantina scuffle can be found in some of the earliest iterations
of *Star Wars*, making it clear that it was something George Lucas was
imagining for years. The earliest synopsis, dated May 1973, had a version of a
"shabby cantina" with "a laser sword" ending a fight.

FINDING YOUR RELIGION

In the early 2000s, there were several attempts undertaken by *Star Wars* fans to overstuff Census efforts in an attempt to get Jedi Knighthood acknowledged as an official religion. In April 2001, a viral email urged U.K. citizens to enter "Jedi Knight," but census officials knew of this attempt and categorized any such entries as "other." The act of having to accommodate this classification led some news outlets to report this as official recognition. Later that same month, something similar happened in Australia.

WARWICK'S WAR STORIES

Since Warwick Davis's first acting role as Wicket W. Warrick in *Return of the Jedi*, he has played several roles in Lucasfilm productions, including the title role of *Willow* (1988) and the supporting roles of Wald and Weazel in *The Phantom Menace*. He was quick to notice that all his *Star Wars* roles started with the letter "W," and it's a connection that has continued since then. In *The Force Awakens* he plays Wollivan. In *The Last Jedi*, Wodibin. In *Rogue One*, he was Weeteef Cyu-Bee, and in *Solo* he was once again Weazel as well as WG-22, Wamoth, and Wazellman. For *Rise of Skywalker*, his roles include Wizzich Mozzer and Wolentic Dudge.

UNDERCOVER KYLO

On the January 16, 2016, episode of *Saturday Night Live*, host Adam Driver starred as Kylo Ren in a sendup of the reality TV show *Undercover Boss*. The premise: Kylo Ren disguises himself as a First Order underling to understand how the rank-and-file regard him. This involved Adam Driver dressing up as "Matt the Radar Technician." The sketch inspired many Matt the Radar Tech cosplay examples, a look that even works its way into an episode of *Star Wars Resistance* in the second season of the animated series. Adam Driver reprised his role in the bit during his third time hosting SNL in January 2020 for *Undercover Boss: Where Are They Now?*

AND SOMETIMES Y

Technical Name:
Consolidated Koensayr
Manufacturing & Holdings
BTA-NR Y-wing

You Know it As:
Resistance Y-wing fighter

Size Specs:
18.2 meters long; 8.8 meter-
wingspan; 2.3 meters tall

Weaponry:
• Two forward-facing Taim
& Bak IX8 laser cannons
• Two turret-mounted ArMek
SW-9 ion cannons
• Two Krupx MG12
warhead launchers

Key Features:
• Armored cockpit module
• Astromech unit
• Customizable hull
configurations

Y-wings have defended the stars since the Clone Wars, being one of the most venerable designs still in operation at the time of the Resistance. The wishbone-shaped fighters made up some of the first fighters used by the Rebel Alliance. The latest models build on that design legacy, featuring some of the systems that Rebel technicians improvised to improve the Clone Wars-era craft. After the fall of the Empire, Y-wing fighters were frequently used by local systems to protect their territories. Some have even fallen into the hands of nefarious scoundrels like the Spice Runners of Kijimi.

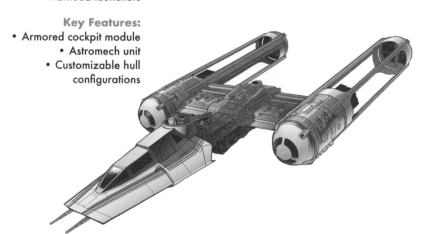

FINDING THE MAESTRO

When George Lucas was looking for a composer for his 1977 space opera, his friend Steven Spielberg recommended John Williams. Although the trend for science-fiction scores at the time was for modern sounds, rock beats, and electronic touches, Lucas wanted a traditional, almost Wagnerian classic score, with grand fanfares and themes for each of the characters. Williams delivered in spades, and the *Star Wars* album became the most popular soundtrack of the time.

THE SUNKEN
DEATH STAR

The idea of exploring the sunken remains of the Death Star and the Emperor's throne room specifically dates back to art explorations done for *The Force Awakens*. Although such a notion was cut early from the story exploration of Episode VII, the visuals had an impact on director J.J. Abrams and he returned their inclusion in *The Rise of Skywalker*. The ruins are on Kef Bir, a moon in the Endor system. The exterior lightsaber duel between Kylo and Rey was shot on chilly days in November and December at the paddock tank at Pinewood Studios.

GEONOSIS

Galactic Placement:
Outer Rim Territories

Star:
Ea, a red star

Orbital Placement:
Second planet from the sun

Terrain:
Harsh rocky desert and dunes

Size:
11,370 kilometers in diameter

Moons:
4 plus a ring system

Length of Day:
30 standard hours

Length of Year:
256 local days

What to Bring:
• Anti-radiation gear. Geonosis is pelted by harsh stellar and cosmic radiation, driving most of its life beneath the surface.

What Happened Here?
• The leaders of the Separatist Alliance sign a treaty to wage war against the Republic.
• Hundreds of Jedi die in the Geonosis execution arena.
• Boba Fett witnesses the death of his father, Jango Fett.
• Anakin loses an arm in duel with Count Dooku.
• The Clone Wars start.
• The Death Star undergoes secret development; to keep the battle station's existence classified, the Empire exterminates the Geonosians.

SOLO PERFORMANCE

In 1975, Harrison Ford was doing some carpentry work at the Los Angeles offices of American Zoetrope, where George Lucas was auditioning actors for the parts in his new film, *Star Wars*. Lucas asked Ford to help out by reading dialogue opposite aspiring actors. At the time, Lucas had been considering a number of actors for the role of Han Solo, including Kurt Russell, Nick Nolte, and Christopher Walken. But when Ford read the Han Solo lines, Lucas realized he was perfect for the role.

TWO NEW STOPS
ON THE TOUR

With each of the new saga films, the Star Tours – The Adventure Continues attraction had added a planet to their itinerary. *The Force Awakens* brought a detour to Jakku, while *The Last Jedi* had a visit to Crait. *The Rise of Skywalker* brings two new destinations: the oceanic moon of Kef Bir, home to an enormous chunk of Death Star wreckage, and the shadowy Sith world of Exegol. The latter bridges a connection with the film because the Starspeeder is one of the many vessels flying about in the end air battle, with Star Tours providing the vantage point from within the commuter shuttle.

REALIZING A
JEDI MASTER

A key VFX challenge for ILM was turning the beloved character of Yoda—which until Episode II was a puppet controlled by Frank Oz—into an all-CG character. ILM Animation Supervisor Rob Coleman closely examined Frank Oz's performances, since he did not want the digital incarnation to seem too far removed from the limitations inherent in a puppet. "The mouth on the Yoda puppet doesn't articulate much," Coleman said. "He couldn't form vowels and phonemes and look like he was really talking—but everyone thought he did! Even I had a flawed memory of what I thought I saw in 1980." The challenge was creating what people thought they remembered, rather than being a direct replication of the puppet's performance.

WHEN IT
SANDSTORMS...

Breaking the curse of inclement weather during the first week of production that hindered *Star Wars* and *The Empire Strikes Back*, *Return of the Jedi* began principal photography indoors, on Stage Two at Elstree Studios on January 11, 1982. There, enormous fans created an indoor sandstorm for a scene (scene #44) that was set on Tatooine. Ironically, all this effort was for naught—the sandstorm scene was the first major scene to be cut from the edit of *Return of the Jedi*.

THE WEAPON OF A JEDI

Technical Name:
Not applicable; this is a handcrafted item

You Know it As:
The Skywalker lightsaber

Size Specs:
24 centimeters long handle; with blade extended, 110 centimeters long

When It Was Made:
During the Clone Wars. Anakin Skywalker was forced to create a new lightsaber after losing one in a Geonosian droid factory.

Key Features:
A scintillating white-blue blade produced by a bonded kyber crystal; blade adjustment knob; D-shaped ring for belt-attachment.

Who's Had It (a partial list):
Anakin Skywalker, Hondo Ohnaka (briefly), General Grievous (briefly), Obi-Wan Kenobi, Luke Skywalker, Han Solo (guts a tauntaun), R2-D2 (for safekeeping) Maz Kanata (likewise), Finn (briefly), Rey.

A lightsaber is an ancient design that serves as a symbol and weapon of the Jedi Knights. At its heart it is a bonded kyber crystal, a glassy stone that, when attuned to the Force by a Jedi in an ancient process called the Gathering, has the ability to amplify the power of an energy cell into a beam of plasma energy and contain it in a permeable, blade-like field. Anyone can use a lightsaber, but the extreme danger posed by a blade that can cut through anything means a Force-user has an advantage in sensing the weapon.

PRE-SHOOTING THE PREQUELS

In the case of *The Phantom Menace*, the filmmakers greatly relied on the utility of animatics, a sort of low-resolution placeholder version of computer animation and quickly assembled video photography to previsualize scenes as the movie was being conceived. These were vital, as upwards of 70 percent of the film would require visual effects work, and decisions needed to be made early to focus that work as effectively as possible. Co-editor Ben Burtt and animatic supervisor David Dozoretz essentially "pre-shot" the movie, with crude temporary CG graphics and footage of crewmembers standing in as characters. This version of Episode I was then replaced bit by bit in editorial as finished shots came in.

REAL-TIME PHASMA

At the 2018 Games Developers Conference in San Francisco, a collaboration between NVIDIA and ILMxLAB showcased the power of real-time rendering. The all-computer-generated short had stormtroopers in a First Order base chatting and snapping to attention as the highly reflective Captain Phasma arrives on scene. With absolute photo-realism, the crowning achievement is not that it is computer rendered. It's that it is computer-rendered live. The camera could be moved in real-time and still produce photo-real imagery. These kind of breakthroughs will greatly inform the future of games and visual effects.

ERNIE THE GREATER

Ernie Fosselius made a name for himself in *Star Wars* circles by making what many consider to be granddaddy of all *Star Wars* fan films, the 1978 satirical parody *Hardware Wars*. The ingenuity displayed in that production earned him contact with those within Lucasfilm, and he became friends with sound designer Ben Burtt. Burtt cast Fosselius as the sobbing rancor keeper in *Return of the Jedi* and considered him his secret weapon in making Poggle the Lesser speak in *Attack of the Clones*. A gifted mimic, Fosselius imitated the sound of his own voice played backward, which was then actually played backward. He added vocal clicks and buzzing noises made by humming on wax paper, creating a distinctive sound for the Geonosian archduke.

OBI-WAN KENOBI'S TIMELINE

Born on Stewjon; brought into the Jedi Order at an early age. In his teens is apprenticed to Qui-Gon Jinn.

Age 15: Obi-Wan and his master Qui-Gon attend to young Duchess Satine Kryze on Mandalore.

Age 25: Accompanies Qui-Gon on mission to Naboo. Witnesses his master slain by Sith Lord Darth Maul.

Age 25: Defeats Maul and presumes him to be dead. Ascends to Jedi Knight and takes Anakin Skywalker as apprentice.

Age 35: Discovers a clone army on Kamino secretly developed for the Jedi.

Age 35: Becomes a general in the Grand Army of the Republic.

Age 37: Faces a resurrected Maul, who slays Duchess Satine in a bid for vengeance.

Age 38: Loses his former Padawan Anakin Skywalker to the dark side; is forced to maim his friend in a duel on Mustafar.

Age 38: Goes into exile on Tatooine, delivering Anakin's son, Luke, to the Lars Homestead.

Age 55: Once again confronts Maul, now an aged Sith broken by the desire for vengeance. Slays the dark warrior.

Age 57: Receives from Luke a distress signal from Princess Leia of Alderaan. Begins teaching Luke the ways of the Force.

Age 57: Aboard the Death Star, confronts Darth Vader. Vader strikes Kenobi down. Obi-Wan becomes one with the Force.

SPACE NOUVEAU

For *The Phantom Menace*, Lucas asked concept artist Iain McCaig and costume designer Trisha Biggar to dress the people of Theed on Naboo in the "clothing of paradise." McCaig's conceptual design for Queen Amidala combined aspects of Pre-Raphaelite paintings and art nouveau with Tibetan and Mongolian ceremonial vestments.

"X" MARKS THE STARFIGHTER

Technical Name:
Incom T-65B Space
Superiority Starfighter

You Know it As:
X-wing fighter

Size Specs:
13.4 meters long;
11.8-meter wingspan

Performance:
Sublight speed of
100 MGLT; atmospheric
airspeed of 1,050 kph

Weaponry:
• Four wingtip-mounted Taim &
Bak KX9 laser cannons
• Two fuselage-mounted Krupx
MG7 proton torpedo launchers

Key Features:
• S-foils that deploy in
X-formation to spread
out weapons and deflector
shield coverage
• Hyperdrive systems
coordinated by an astromech
droid in rear socket

The X-wing traces its design origins to the ARC-170 and Z-95 Headhunter fighters used by the Galactic Republic in the Clone Wars. It was set to become the signature fighter of the Empire, but the Imperial Navy went in a different direction. Imperial brass, obsessed with bigger and bigger shows of power, preferred huge warships that carried smaller craft that were dependent on the fleet for launch, so there was no place for this cutting-edge hyperdrive-equipped fighter in the Empire. Luckily for the galaxy, these designs worked their way into the Rebel Alliance's forces. The X-wing became the spear that pierced the armor of the seemingly unstoppable Death Stars—twice!—and were instrumental in the Rebellion's defeat of the Galactic Empire.

ALL'S FAIR
IN *STAR WARS*

With each of the prequels, and each film of the latest trilogy, world-renowned photographer Annie Leibovitz has visited the set and captured candid and arresting moments with her camera, offering a unique look at each film that would be showcased in a special issue of *Vanity Fair*. "I've always been in love with [the filmmaking] process," Leibovtiz said. "I cannot walk on a film set today without being enamored with the way these things are done. I'm so lucky to be able to observe people like George Lucas and J.J. Abrams, who are literally geniuses. I always have to say to *Vanity Fair*, 'How many pages do we have?'"

IN THE BEGINNING

George Lucas began writing Episode I on November 1, 1994. It was then titled "The Beginning." As he did with his previous screenplays, he wrote it out longhand on yellow note paper. Originally slated as a 1997 release, Episode I would grow and evolve in the telling such that its release date was revised to 1999.

THE MUPPET CONNECTION

Frank Oz was the voice and puppeteer of both Miss Piggy and Yoda. Mark Hamill (Luke Skywalker) was a big fan of the Muppets, so when Oz arrived on set, Hamill begged him to do his Miss Piggy voice, but Oz refused. A week later, during rehearsals, Oz was hidden underneath the set, holding up the Yoda puppet, which was "talking" to Luke. "Follow your feelings, you must," Yoda said. Luke responded, "I *am* following my feelings!" Just then, right next to Yoda, up popped Miss Piggy, who exclaimed, "You want feelings? I'll show you feelings, punk! What is this hole? I've been booked in some dumps before, but never like this. Get me my agent on the phone!"

WIN, LOSE, OR TIE

Technical Name:
Sienar Fleet Systems TIE/ln
space superiority starfighter

You Know it As:
TIE fighter

Size Specs:
8.8 meters tall;
7.2 meters long

Performance:
Sublight speed of
100 MGLT; atmospheric
airspeed of 1,200 kph

Weaponry:
• Two "chin" mounted
SFS L-s1 laser cannons

Key Features:
• Hexagonal stellar
energy collectors
• Lightweight construction
allows for extreme
maneuverability
• Twin ion engines

Buzzing about Imperial installations or flitting between their enormous warships are gnat-like TIE fighters, the standard fighter-craft of the Imperial Navy. The single-seater short-range vessel lacks a hyperdrive, requiring deployment from launch bases and carrier ships. TIEs are typically employed en masse to overwhelm enemy ships in number. Speedy and maneuverable, these fighters are nonetheless fragile. Although hard to hit, even a glancing blow can destroy a TIE. The Imperial TIE series draws inspiration from the Jedi interceptors unveiled late in the Clone Wars, as well as support fighters like the V-wing series. Future TIE models—those used by the First Order—would incorporate combat shields and hyperdrive systems.

AGE OF
EMPERORS

Building off the Emperor's brief appearance as a hologram in *The Empire Strikes Back*, the filmmakers knew they would need to recast the role for his featured appearance in *Return of the Jedi*. It was known the Emperor appeared old and crone-like, so some of the contenders for the role were older men in their seventies. Ian McDiarmid, who got the part, was not yet forty when he played Palpatine. His natural age utterly disappeared under Nick Dudman's extensive makeup. His young-playing-old was quite beneficial for him nearly fifteen years later, when he played a more age-appropriate incarnation of Senator Palpatine in *Star Wars*: Episode I *The Phantom Menace*.

CONNECTING
THROUGH THE FORCE

The course of action in *The Last Jedi* required Kylo Ren and Rey to be apart, but through the Force—and editing—they continued to be connected. "Design-wise with the Force connections, I didn't want it to be about some kind of trippy effect of them connecting across the universe," said writer-director Rian Johnson. "I wanted it to be just as intimate and simple as possible." Editor Bob Ducsay simply cut the scenes as if the actors were in the same room together, even though they were shot in different environments (the off-camera actor was on-set, however). In this way, the oldest trick in cinema—making separate moments feel unified—created the Force magic.

COME
SAIL AWAY

Technical Name:
Ubrikkian LO-KD57
luxury barge

You Know it As:
Jabba's sail barge

Size:
26.3 meters long,
9.5 meters tall

Performance:
100 kph top speed

Weaponry:
• Removable rail-mounted CEC
Gi/9 antipersonnel
blaster cannons (variable
number; typically 20)
• CEC Me/7 heavy custom-
mounted double laser cannon

Key Features:
• Observation lounge
with PA system
• Triple-thrust turbines and
fabric sails for powered or
unpowered propulsion
• Adjustable window shutters

Known as the *Khetanna*, the sail barge employed by Jabba the Hutt suited his outsized tastes for splendor and relaxation. Jabba led expeditions into the desert aboard his sail barge when his business dealings called for the elimination of rivals or partners in the Great Pit of Carkoon. On the day he sought to feed Luke Skywalker to the almighty Sarlacc, Jabba discovered the hard way that Jedi aren't all that easy to swallow. Luke embarked on a one-man assault that cut through most of Jabba's guards, allowing him access to the top deck of the barge, and the turret cannon found there. Luke fired the cannon into the deck, setting off a chain reaction of explosions that consumed the barge.

I'M LUKE STARKILLER.
I'M HERE TO RESCUE YOU.

In early drafts of the script, George Lucas planned to portray Luke Skywalker as an elderly general, but he decided that making him a teenager gave him more potential for character development. Lucas originally named the character Luke Starkiller, but on the first day of shooting, he changed it to the less violent Luke Skywalker.

COLBERT GREENSCREEN
CHALLENGE

On August 10, 2006, Stephen Colbert, then host of *The Colbert Report*, did a segment on his show where he clumsily re-enacted some lightsaber moves while standing against a greenscreen. The footage went viral in the early days of YouTube, as fans began replacing the background with a variety of *Star Wars* and non-*Star Wars* themed menaces. Colbert ran with the gag and began showcasing some of the more creative entries on his show. This culminated in The Green Screen Challenge and an entry delivered by none other than George Lucas (which featured ILM visual effects and a cameo by Jar Jar Binks, voiced by Ahmed Best). True to the spirit of the show, Lucas came in second.

TATOOINE

Galactic Placement:
Outer Rim Territories

Stars:
Tatoo I and Tatoo II, binary
yellow stars

Orbital Placement:
First from the suns

Terrain:
Sand (it gets everywhere)

Size:
10,465 kilometers

Moons:
3

Length of Day:
23 standard hours

Length of Year:
304 local days

What to Bring:
• Very strong sunscreen. These
double stars will age your skin!
• As much water as you can haul.
Consider bringing a portable
moisture vaporator to condense
moisture from the air.

What Happened Here?
• Anakin Skywalker was
discovered by the Jedi.
• Obi-Wan Kenobi lived in exile.
• Luke Skywalker was raised
to be a great pilot.
• Jabba the Hutt lived large.

THE AGE OF ANAKIN

The story of Episode I would always center on Anakin Skywalker in his youth, but his age would fluctuate as George Lucas developed the story. Some approaches favored him closer to his early teen years, while others had him younger. In the end, Lucas decided age nine was ideal, as the impact of the boy's separation from his mother needed to cast a long shadow on the rest of Anakin's life.

MAILING THE
DEATH STAR PLANS

To mark the 30th anniversary of *Star Wars*, the United States Postal Service released a series of fifteen commemorative forty-one-cent stamps featuring *Star Wars* characters, vehicles, and scenes designed by Drew Struzan. Furthermore, the USPS decorated some 400 mailboxes across the US to resemble R2-D2, prompting a rash of Princess Leia cosplayers to re-enact the depositing of the Death Star plans into the little droid.

THE BIG REVEAL
STAR WARS: THE EMPIRE STRIKES BACK

INT. GANTRY - OUTSIDE CONTROL ROOM - REACTOR SHAFT

                    VADER
There is no escape. Don't make me destroy you. You
do not yet realize your importance. You have only
begun to discover your power. Join me and I will
complete your training. With our combined strength,
we can end this destructive conflict and bring order
                to the galaxy.

                    LUKE
             I'll never join you!

                    VADER
If you only knew the power of the dark side.
Obi-Wan never told you what happened to your
                    father.

                    LUKE
He told me enough! It was you who killed him.

                    VADER
            No. I am your father.

Shocked, Luke looks at Vader in utter disbelief.

                    LUKE
No. No. That's not true! That's impossible!

                    VADER
Search your feelings. You know it to be true.

LUKE
No! No! No!

VADER
Luke. You can destroy the Emperor. He has foreseen
this. It is your destiny. Join me, and together we
can rule the galaxy as father and son. Come with
me. It is the only way.

Vader puts away his sword and holds his hand out
to Luke.

A calm comes over Luke, and he makes a decision.
In the next instant he steps off the gantry platform
into space. The Dark Lord looks over the platform
and sees Luke falling far below. The wind begins to
blow at Vader's cape and the torrent finally forces
him back, away from the edge. The wind soon fades and
the wounded Jedi begins to drop fast, unable to grab
onto anything to break his fall.

The shooting script for this scene had Vader say to Luke that "Ben killed your
father." Mark Hamill knew the true line though, having been informed by
director Irvin Kershner prior to shooting.

THE KNIGHTS OF
REN RETURN

Briefly seen in a flashback sequence in *The Force Awakens*, the Knights of Ren would get their due screen time in *The Rise of Skywalker*. Played by stunt performers, the Knights would have no dialogue and would instead let their imposing costumes and props and combat style do their talking for them. The Knights were a relatively late addition to *The Force Awakens*, and their abbreviated time on screen meant their costumes were completed only to the level required for the shots. For their extended role in Episode IX, their costumes were rebuilt to hold up to more scrutiny and more details were added.

A NEW FORCE
AT BREAKFAST

Add breakfast cereal spokesdroid to C-3PO's list of secondary functions: in 1984, Kellogg's brought C-3PO's to the supermarket, a golden brand of "crunchy honey-sweetened oat, wheat and corn cereal." The campaign included national TV spots starring C-3PO and R2-D2 in a rare live-action outing after the original trilogy, with Anthony Daniels reprising his role as C-3PO. No one is quite sure what the cereal shapes—squarish number eights—are meant to represent. Are they the tabs that stick out from the side of C-3PO's head where ears would be? We may never know; the cereal line did not last long.

QUITE THE FLEX

None of the spaceship models ever moved an inch during the filming of the flight sequences. The motion was an optical illusion created by moving the cameras around motionless models. The visual effects team custom hardwired a computer to an old Vista Vision camera to create a motion-control system that was dubbed the Dykstraflex, named after Industrial Light & Magic's first visual effects supervisor John Dykstra. The Dykstraflex camera was attached to the end of a boom arm and could be programmed to pan, tilt, pass, and track around a model positioned before a blue screen.

LIKE EWOK,
LIKE WOKLING

Warwick Davis played the role of Wicket W. Warrick when he was 11 years old for *Return of the Jedi*. For a brief cameo in *The Rise of Skywalker*, he reprised his first on-screen role and passed the tradition onto his son, Harrison, who joined him in Ewok costume to play Wicket's son, Pommet. "Wicket has indeed produced an offspring," said Warwick. "He's older and wiser and he has a little scamp to handle now."

LEIA ORGANA'S TIMELINE

- **Born** on Polis Massa along with twin brother Luke to Padmé Amidala; adopted by Bail and Breha Organa of Alderaan

- **Age 16:** Leia undergoes the Day of Demand, a traditional Alderaanian ritual to demonstrate her fitness to rule on the throne someday.

- **Age 19:** As custodian of the stolen Death Star plans from the Battle of Scarif, Senator Leia Organa is captured by Darth Vader.

- **Age 19:** Leia is forced to witness the Death Star destroy Alderaan as Grand Moff Tarkin tries to force her to reveal the rebel base location.

- **Age 19:** Leia assists in her own rescue by Han Solo and Luke Skywalker and escapes the Death Star with the plans needed to destroy the station.

- **Age 22:** After the rebels are scattered by the Empire from their base on Hoth, Leia falls in love with Han Solo.

- **Age 23:** Leia slays Jabba the Hutt, joins the Endor strike team that helps destroy the Death Star, and celebrates the fall of the Empire.

- **Age 23:** Aware that Luke is her brother, Leia begins Jedi training. She hangs up the lightsaber when it's clear her life will follow a different path.

- **Age 24:** Leia gives birth to Ben Solo.

- **Age 47:** Leia leaves politics behind to focus on forming and leading a Resistance to face the growing threat of the First Order.

- **Age 53:** Leia is nearly killed when blown into space during a First Order ambush on the Resistance cruiser *Raddus*.

- **Age 54:** Leia leads a final effort against the First Order, particularly when word spreads that the Emperor has somehow returned.

MUSICAL
FORESHADOWING

Young Anakin Skywalker's musical theme, featured in *The Phantom Menace* as a bright, hopeful, and earnest example of music does have a dark underpinning: a segment of the Imperial March, Darth Vader's theme, can be quietly heard amid the gentle melody. "'Anakin's Theme' definitely includes a series of musical clues that people might recognize as the music of someone else we've already encountered," composer John Williams said. For those who sat through the end credits of Episode I to fully appreciate Williams's score, there was an extra hint of what was to come—the final sound over black as the credits conclude is the sound of Vader breathing.

WHERE THE GRAYS COME FROM

The Kaminoans closely resemble the aliens of UFO conspiracy culture, the so-called "Grays" that the U.S. government is supposedly holding prisoner at Area 51 and who are responsible for a rash of abductions and cattle mutilations and other odd occurances in fringe folklore. George Lucas specifically requested the look as a nod to that mythology and an homage to his pal Steven Spielberg's *Close Encounters of the Third Kind*. He envisioned them hailing from an oceanic world, as the ocean is the cradle of all life. "They are recreating life there," he said, "and Kaminoans are creatures that began life in the sea."

DIGITAL CINEMA
REVOLUTION

For *Star Wars*: Episode II *Attack of the Clones*, George Lucas and producer Rick McCallum worked with Sony for six years to design the perfect cameras—the HDW-F900 24-P—to shoot this movie. The partnership included Panavision, which would develop lenses for the camera to meet the needs of cinematographers. The entire project was shot, processed, edited, and even distributed (by satellite download) and projected digitally in some markets. When Episode I opened, there were four digital screens. When Episode II opened on May 16, 2002, about one hundred of its 3,161 theaters had digital screens. Now, that number of digital screens available tops 38,000.

SLEEK, SOPHISTICATED STYLE

Technical Name:
Theed Palace Space Vessel Engineering Corps N-1

You Know it As:
Naboo starfighter

Size Specs:
11 meters long

Performance:
Sublight speed of 100 MGLT; atmospheric speed of 1,100 kph

Weaponry:
- Two forward-facing laser cannons
- One nose-mounted proton torpedo launcher

Key Features:
- Royal chromium-capped sublight thrusters
- Clean-burning ion engines

A throwback to a more handcrafted era, the Naboo starfighter is a far cry from the machine-stamped, mass-produced war machines of the Galactic Civil War era. Naboo artisans and technicians take care and pride in the artistry of their designs, producing a sleek, polished vessel of precision engineering. Rather than betray the deliberate profile of the ship by making the astromech droid socket larger to accommodate standard sizes, R2 units and similar must compress their body shells to fit within the confines of the N-1 starfighter's shape. The long "rat-tail" finial trailing from the ship is a power charge collector that plugs into energizer sockets that line the Naboo Royal Hangar.

JOURNEYS INTO
READING

Accompanying each of the new *Star Wars* films has been a publishing program dubbed the "Journey to" program. Separate from novelizations or adaptations of the cinematic content, these books are prequels or tie-ins that expand the content in ways big and small. Noteworthy in *The Journey to The Force Awakens* were stories set in the original trilogy era that would lay the foundation of what would come. The Battle of Jakku that littered the desert with wrecked ships was featured in, for example, the *Lost Stars* novel. For *The Last Jedi* lead-in, Captain Phasma's backstory was revealed in an eponymous novel; for *The Rise of Skywalker*, the efforts to rebuild the Resistance was featured in books like *Resistance Reborn*.

THE LOOK OF VADER

George Lucas told concept artist Ralph McQuarrie that Darth Vader should be a tall, black, majestic figure with fluttering robes, possibly wearing an exotic helmet, like a Japanese warrior, with a black silk scarf across his face. Studying the original script, McQuarrie noted that Vader first appeared when he jumped from one spaceship to another, so Lucas agreed he should wear a breathing apparatus.

THRONE OF THE SITH

The jagged Sith throne found deep beneath Exegol in *The Rise of Skywalker* finds its origins in artwork by Ralph McQuarrie exploring an idea from the early drafts of *Return of the Jedi*. In that version of Episode VI, the Emperor ruled from a throne room hidden deep beneath the surface of Had Abbadon, the city planet. That throne sat in a pool of lava.

CRUMB
STEALS THE SHOW

Salacious B. Crumb, the cackling Kowakian monkey-lizard that sits by Jabba's tail, was a character whose role kept growing as puppeteer Tim Rose brought more and more life to the part. Originally scripted only for one scene wherein two aliens aboard the sail barge have an argument, and Salacious sits on one of their shoulders goading them on, Crumb's role expanded to be Jabba's pet and jester. Crumb even unofficially "co-hosted" several made-for-television behind-the-scenes documentaries that accompanied the film, such as *From Star Wars to Jedi* and *Classic Creatures*. Crumb was sculpted by Tony McVey, who returned to the design to create more monkey-lizards for *The Mandalorian* TV series.

DARK COMPASS

Technical Name:
Not applicable; this is a handcrafted item

You Know it As:
Sith wayfinder

Size Specs:
It fits in the palm of a hand

Key Features:
• Supralight loadstone
• Plasmatic interior harvested from deep space nebulae

These pyramidal trinkets resemble Sith holocrons and are etched with Sith runes that give them a sinister appearance. These are ancient devices that were used before the advent of modern hyperspace navigation and effectively function as compasses in space, attuned to a specific world. In this manner, the ancient Sith were able to find their strongholds, whereas the Jedi could not follow. Kylo Ren used a wayfinder recovered from Darth Vader's castle on Mustafar to locate the planet Exegol.

CREATING ILM

While preparing for *Star Wars* in 1975, George Lucas investigated existing optical facilities but could not find a special-effects company equipped to do what he wanted. So Lucas started his own! Initially founded to work solely on *Star Wars*, Industrial Light & Magic (ILM) combined new technology with old techniques to create stunning visual effects and went on to produce groundbreaking work for more than 200 features, as well as TV, theme park attractions, and more.

SEE-THROUGH-PIO

The early, skeletal incarnation of C-3PO seen in *The Phantom Menace* is a good example of collaboration between old and new methods. At the time in the late 1990s, a skeletal C-3PO would be too complex to build as a CG animated character but was also impossible to realize as a man in a suit. Instead, C-3PO was built as a practical puppet by the ILM Model Shop and puppeteered in the bunraku style, a 17th-century Japanese technique wherein the puppeteer stands behind the model and drives its performance. ILM artists then digitally painted out the puppeteer, replacing the performer with imagery from a "clean plate" version of the empty set.

THE COMPOSITE
GRIEVOUS

Australian actor Duncan Young read Grievous's parts on the Episode III set (indeed, he read all the CG character parts), providing the needed cues for the actors working opposite him. For combat scenes, stunt performer Kyle Rowling would play the role, dressed in a snug blue or green bodysuit. But when it came time to cast Grievous, that journey took longer than expected. Ben Burtt recorded a temporary track in the edit, and there were attempts to fill the role with a big name. In the end, it was supervising sound editor (and trained actor) Matthew Wood who got the part. He snuck in an audition under a fake name (A. Smithee) and it was the one George Lucas selected.

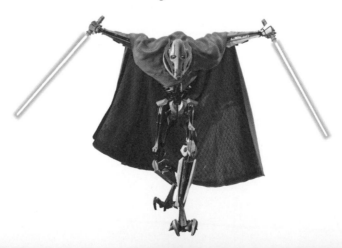

MUSTAFAR

Galactic Placement:
Outer Rim Territories

Star:
Priate, a red star

Orbital Placement:
Third planet from the sun,
overlapping orbit

Terrain:
Mountains, volcanoes,
caves, lava floes

Size:
4,200 kilometers in diameter

Moons:
0

Length of Day:
36 standard hours

Length of Year:
412 local days

What to Bring:
• Fireproof everything.
Windswept embers, dry
conditions, and lava
eruptions make for extremely
flammable conditions.
• Air supply. Not only
chilled air to help keep from
overheating, but fresh air,
as the ash and contaminants
make some areas of Mustafar
impossible to breathe in.

What Happened Here?
• The Separatist council is
wiped out by Darth Vader.
• Anakin—as Darth Vader—
duels his former master
Obi-Wan Kenobi and is
horribly wounded and burned.
• Darth Vader has
a castle there.

JAR JAR'S
PLACEHOLDER TITLE

As a seemingly wry acknowledgment to the pointedly divisive opinions garnered by the floppy-eared Gungan sidekick of *The Phantom Menace*, George Lucas began writing the screenplay for Episode II with the placeholder name *Jar Jar's Great Adventure*. Even the animatic version of the famous opening crawl had this title underneath the "Episode" number.

CANDID
WEBCAM MOMENTS

Episode III took the unusual step of having a webcam on set to transmit images live (granted, at one frame every twenty seconds or so) to members of a StarWars.com subscription service. Given the amount of downtime on a movie set, waiting for a setup to be ready, the camera became a curiosity to crew members and a way to directly communicate to the *Star Wars* fan community. Highlights included Ewan McGregor and Hayden Christensen wanting to show off their stunt practice on camera, George Lucas showing off Christensen's Episode III look by pointing the camera to an HD monitor, and ILM supervisor John Knoll directing time-lapse animation by moving objects between the long gaps of frame refreshes.

CANTINA CREATURES

The Mos Eisley Cantina sequence was originally shot at Elstree Studios in April of 1976, with a gaggle of creatures delivered by Stuart Freeborn's creature shop. The assortment of aliens failed to live up to George Lucas's active imagination, so a mere four months before the movie's release, he scheduled an additional stint of photography in Los Angeles to fill in booths and cutaways to even more outlandish aliens, created by Industrial Light & Magic and creature maestro Rick Baker. The end sequence is a seamless, skillful blending of both U.K. and U.S. photography through editorial tricks.

HOUSING A
STAR DESTROYER

There are few places that can house a Star Destroyer—or rather an extended section of Star Destroyer hull. To film the valiant orbak charge on the surface of a First Order command ship, the Episode IX crew filmed at the Cardington Air Sheds, a former Royal Air Force site that housed enormous dirigibles and research balloons. It had previously been used to represent the Yavin 4 Rebel base in the original *Star Wars* as well as *Rogue One: A Star Wars Story*.

THE FETT FAMILY RIDE

Technical Name:
Modified Kuat Systems Engineering *Firespray*-class patrol and attack ship

You Know it As:
Slave I

Size Specs:
21.5 meters long; 21.3 meter wingspan

Performance:
Sublight speed of 70 MGLT; atmospheric airspeed of 1,000 kph

Weaponry:
- Two midship blaster cannons
- Two trunk-mounted laser cannons
- Two recessed missile launchers
- One aft seismic charge mine layer
- Other rumored nasty surprises

Key Features:
- Sensor-baffling stealth array
- Concealed weapons systems

The pride and joy of Jango Fett during his bounty-hunting career, the *Slave I* is an exensively modified Firespray patrol ship loaded with weaponry in a frequently changing configuration. After Jango's untimely death at Geonosis, young Boba inherited the craft, though he had older hunters like Aurra Sing and Bossk do the flying while he grew up. For a time, it belonged to Hondo Ohnaka, who repainted it, before returning once more to Boba Fett's possession.

THE MIRROR CAVE

The mirror cave sequence was one of the earliest Rian Johnson had while developing the story of *The Last Jedi* as a way of symbolizing Rey's quest for identity. VFX studio One of Us devised the sequence by shooting Daisy Ridley with a multi-digital camera rig offset in space and time so that one take could ripple through multiple images of Rey. In saving resources while making the movie, the mirror cave environment also doubled for the interior of the Jedi temple and boulder cave at the back of the mining tunnels on Crait.

TALL DRINK OF VADER

David Prowse is a six-foot-six, 266-pound former heavyweight wrestling champion. George Lucas saw him in *A Clockwork Orange* (1971) and offered him his choice between two parts: Chewbacca or Vader. Prowse chose Vader because he didn't like the idea of going around in a "gorilla suit" for six months. James Earl Jones (Darth Vader's voice) and David Prowse (who played him onscreen) have never met.

THE MAESTRO'S CAMEO

After his inestimable contributions to the *Star Wars* legacy through his nine music scores that shape that saga, John Williams finally appeared on screen in *The Rise of Skywalker* in a brief cameo as Oma Tres (an anagram of "Maestro"), a tinkerer on Kijimi. In the film, he is surrounded by props meant to symbolize each of the fifty-one movie scores that have earned him an Oscar nomination—a literal hook for *Hook*, a series of yellow canisters to represent the buoys in *Jaws*, and a cable coiled like Indiana Jones' bullwhip in *Raiders of the Lost Ark*, to name a few.

HAN SOLO'S TIMELINE

Born on Corellia; Han does not talk about his past very often—and even less about his parents.

Age 8: Han joins a gang of scrumrats in the Corellian slums run by Lady Proxima and the White Worms

Age 19: Han steals from the White Worms and tries—but fails—to get off-planet with his girlfriend Q'ira.

Age 19: Separated from Q'ira, Han joins the Imperial Navy and studies at the Academy on Carida.

Age 22: Washed out of the Navy, Han becomes a mudtrooper grunt slogging through trench warfare on Mimban.

Age 22: Han meets Chewbacca and, with his mentor Tobias Beckett, hires Lando Calrissian to make a Kessel Run.

Age 22: Han wins the *Millennium Falcon* from Lando in a cutthroat sabacc game.

Age 32: After having to dump cargo belonging to Jabba the Hutt, Han needs money, so he takes on a charter to Alderaan.

Age 32: Han joins up with the rebels and meets Princess Leia. It's love at first fight.

Age 35: Han is captured by bounty hunter Boba Fett and frozen in carbonite for delivery to Jabba.

Age 36: Thawed from his frozen hell, Han is reunited with Leia and becomes a general in the Rebel Alliance.

Age 66: Han is slain by Kylo Ren while trying to reach out to Ben, his son beneath Ren's dark mask.

ENDOR
WILDLIFE

A close look at the Ewok village sequences in *Return of the Jedi* reveals some rather terrestrial creatures living among the trees. A flock of twelve chickens (at least, that's the number according to the call sheets) were on set in the village square and can be seen in some establishing shots. Look to Chief Chirpa and you'll see an iguana crawling on him as he deliberated the fates of the heroes. According to the novelization of *Return of the Jedi*, the iguana is Chirpa's "pet and advisor."

WALKING TALL

Technical Name:
Kuat Drive Yards All Terrain
Armored Transport

You Know it As:
AT-AT walker

Size Specs:
25.9 meters long,
22.2 meters tall

Performance:
60 kph over even terrain

Weaponry:
• Two "chin"-mounted Taim &
Bak MS-1 heavy laser cannons
• Two "temple"-mounted
Taim & Bak FF-4 medium
repeating blasters

Key Features:
• Four plodding feet moved
about by powerful legs
• Incredibly strong armor
• De-icing systems

Thundering across uneven terrain with plodding steps that shake the landscape are Imperial walkers. The design might seem primitive, but so is the fear they spark in rebel infantry. Their thick armor and powerful weapons let the Empire walk all over the rebel defenses on Hoth, scoring a decisive victory. Their well-documented use on the ice planet led to their nickname "snow walker," as they often take on the name of their deployed environments. AT-ATs are an evolution of war vehicle designs unleashed on the battlefield of Geonosis at the start of the Clone Wars. A number of AT-AT variant exists for specialist mission profiles.

MAY THE "IV"
BE WITH YOU

Now known as Episode IV: *A New Hope*, that title was added to *Star Wars* years after its release, when it was known that the *Star Wars* saga would continue to expand. Its first public unveiling was in the pages of *The Art of Star Wars*, a 1979 Ballantine Books release that included the entire screenplay for *Star Wars*, complete with a title page that identified it as Episode IV: *A New Hope*. This paved the way for *The Empire Strikes Back*'s release, which labeled it as Episode V in the crawl. The proper Episode number would not appear on *Star Wars* until its April 10, 1981, re-release.

JAKKU

Galactic Placement:
Inner Rim, Western Reaches

Star:
Jakku, yellow star

Orbital Placement:
First from the sun

Terrain:
Desert—dunes and canyons

Size:
6,400 kilometers in diameter

Moons:
2

Length of Day:
26.8 standard hours

Length of Year:
315 local days

What to Bring:
• Food—there's not much in terms of natural food there, so bringing your own provisions will not only keep you fed, but any extra can be used to barter.

What Happened?
• A great battle filled the desert with vast fields of wreckage and derelict starships.
• The *Millennium Falcon* comes to rest here as an ill-gotten ship belonging to Unkar Plutt.
• Rey grows up in a life of solitude.
• Finn defects from the First Order after an attack on a civilian village.
• A partial map to Luke Skywalker's location is retrieved from Lor San Tekka and then given to BB-8 for safe keeping.

A NEW VADER
VANTAGE POINT

George Lucas said part of his goal with the creation of the prequel trilogy was to change the audience's perspective of Darth Vader in the first trilogy. "In IV, people didn't know whether Vader was a robot or a monster or if there was anybody in there. This way, when you see him walk into the spaceship in Episode IV, you're going to say, 'Oh, my god, that's Anakin. The poor guy is still stuck in his suit.' So the tension and drama is completely reversed."

WALKING THE WALKERS

The stop-motion animation models of the Imperial AT-ATs in *The Empire Strikes Back* were created by Jon Berg and Tom St. Amand from concept sketches by Joe Johnston. For the prototype, Berg created moving parts that included small squared-off pistons in the upper legs, which made the AT-ATs appear more mechanically operational.

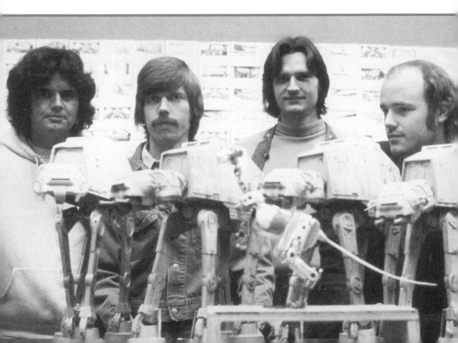

BIKING THROUGH ENDOR

Technical Name:
Aratech 74-Z

You Know it As:
Imperial speeder bike

Size specs:
3.3 meters long

Performance:
Top speed of 500 kph
in short bursts

Weaponry:
• Underslung forward-facing
Ax-20 blaster cannon

Key Features:
• Rocker-pivot foot pedal-
controlled acceleration
• Communications and jammer
suite (center switch)
• Outrigger-mounted
steering vanes

Soaring at amazing speeds on recon and patrol missions, the Aratech 74-Z speeder bike is a slim, single-person repulsorlift vehicle in military service since the Clone Wars. The lightweight bike can attain speeds in excess of 500 kilometers per hour, though only the truly foolhardy would go full speed in occluded terrain conditions. The steering vanes on the long outrigger forks give the speeder bike its maneuverability; should anything happen to these delicate pieces of equipment, the bike is liable to spin madly out of control.

THE LIGHTSABER
CALLS TO YOU

Luke Skywalker's lightsaber—or rather, the "hero" lightsaber prop used for filming in *Star Wars* and *The Empire Strikes Back*—sold for $240,000 at an auction in 2008. The Panavision camera used by director George Lucas while filming *A New Hope* is worth nearly three times as much. When it went up for auction that same year, the camera sold for $625,000, breaking records for both *Star Wars* memorabilia and vintage cameras.

WIN
YODA DOES

The unforgettable moment in *Attack of the Clones* where Yoda brandishes a lightsaber for the first time and shows just what a Jedi Master is capable of garnered an MTV Movie Award nomination for Best Fight, in 2003. It was up against Jet Li versus the Ultimate Fighters in *Cradle 2 the Grave*; Fann Wong versus the palace guards in *Shanghai Knights*; and Johnny Knoxville versus Butterbean in *Jackass: The Movie*. Win, Yoda did, with a newly ILM-animated Yoda acceptance speech voiced by Frank Oz thanks Christopher Lee, Samuel L. Jackson, Natalie Portman, Watto, Chewie, Taun We, Vin Diesel, R2-D2, C-3PO, Björk, Greedo, Steve Guttenberg, Ki-Adi-Mundi, Lama Su, Queen Latifah, and all the younglings at MTV.

THE STARTING GRID
STAR WARS: THE PHANTOM MENACE

EXT. MOS ESPA - DESERT RACE ARENA - DAY
An EXTREME HIGH WIDE ANGLE reveals a vast arena in the Tatooine desert. A large semi-circular amphitheater that holds at least a hundred thousand people dominates the landscape. Large viewing platforms loom over the racetrack.

INT. MOS ESPA — ARENA ANNOUNCER'S BOX — DAY (FX)
A two-headed ANNOUNCER describes the scene.

FODE/BEED

A: Toong mee cha kulkah du Boonta magi, tah oos azalus ooval podraces. (We have perfect weather today for the Boonta Classic. The most hazardous of all podraces.)

B: That's absolutely right. And a big turnout here, from all corners of the Outer Rim territories. I see the contestants are making their way out onto the starting grid.

EXT. MOS ESPA — DESERT RACE ARENA - DAY
On the left side of the tracks across from the grandstands,a line of podracers emerges from the large hangar, surrounded by several CREW MEMBERS. Pods are pulled by a wide variety of CREATURES and are led by aliens carrying flags. The PILOTS stand facing the royal box.

FODE/BEED (O.S.)
A: Ya, yama beestoo (Yes, there they are!)

B: I see Ben Quadinaros from the Tund system.

A: ...eh Gasgano doowa Ord Pedrovia! Ee Boonta go wata Teemto Pagalies!(And Gasgano in his new Ord Pedrovia.)

B: Two-time winner, Boles Roor…

A: Woe granee champion du Pixelito, Sebulba! (On the front line the reigning champion, Sebulba from Pixelito.)

SEBULBA
Godo che!

FODE/BEED (O.S.)
B: And in the front row, nearside pole position, Mawhonic! A hearty hello to Clegg Holdfast in his Voltec K-T-nine Wasp. And back again, it's the mighty Dud Bolt, with that incredible racing machine, the Vulptereen three-two-seven. And hoping for a big win today, Ody Mandrell, with his record-setting pit droid team. And a late entry, young Anakin Skywalker, a local boy. I see the flags are moving out onto the track.

EXT. MOS ESPA - ARENA - GRANDSTAND - DAY
Wide shot of crowd watching flag bearers step onto field and a medium shot of the flag bearers and their flags standing in front of the pods.

––––––

ILM Animators took cues off of real-world actors to inspire the characterizations of the pilots. For example, scrappy Ratts Tyerell was Joe Pesci; gentle giant Ark Bumpy "Roose" was John Goodman; showman Gasgano was Michael York; and the flamboyant Teemto Pagalies was Nathan Lane/Dom DeLuise.

THE SPIRIT OF A JEDI MASTER

Star Wars fan Riley Howell, aged 21, died in April 2019, tackling the shooter at the tragic UNC Charlotte shooting—a brave sacrifice that saved lives. Howell's friends and family would remark in their remembrances of his passion for *Star Wars*, such that a fellow fan reached out to Lucasfilm to memorialize Howell in some way. The matter was kept private until a former high school teacher spotted mention of an ancient Jedi historian, Ri-Lee Howell, in a *Rise of Skywalker* guide book, who was said to be one of the sages who added knowledge to the ancient Jedi texts seen in the film.

CLUBBING ON CORUSCANT

A chase through city planet traffic brings Obi-Wan Kenobi and Anakin Skywalker into a colorful and crowded Coruscant nightclub in Episode II (later called the "Outlander"). This was a rare example of a fully built set on the production, which often relied on partial sets or just expanses of bluescreen for its locations. Every direction one looked within the nightclub set on Stage 3 at Fox Studios Sydney would provide otherworldly scenery. When filled with extras, smoke, and noise, it completed the illusion. But the nightclub only stood half a day, on July 17, 2000. After the club sequence as shot, the crew immediately started tearing it down to build another set needed in production.

A FAMILY PORTRAIT

As George Lucas's last *Star Wars* movie, *Revenge of the Sith* was a chance to place himself and his children into the galaxy he created through a number of brief cameos. Lucas and his daughters share a frame as Coruscant nobles in the hallway outside the opera house theater. George plays a blue-skinned Pantoran named Baron Papanoida, while his daughter Katie plays a similarly hued Senator Chi Eekway. His daughter Amanda plays Senator Terr Taneel. His son Jett had the most visible cameo, as Zett Jukassa, the Padawan who is shot by clone troopers as Bail Organa visits the burning Jedi Temple.

STRANGE ORDER

In the fall of 1978, ILM effects artists Phil Tippett and Lorne Peterson had to scour San Francisco furriers for a most unusual ingredient: tanned unborn calfskin. This would result from calves unknowingly killed during the slaughtering of a female cow. As macabre as it may seem, this fur was the perfect scale for the miniature construction of the stop-motion tauntauns that would appear in the movie. Tom St. Amand and Doug Beswick built the final armature of the puppet that would be animated a frame at a time.

GIMME AN A!

Technical Name:
Kuat Systems
Engineering RZ-1

You Know it As:
A-wing starfighter

Size specs:
6.9 meters long

Performance:
Sublight speed of 120
MGLT; atmospheric
speed of 1,300 kph

Weaponry:
• Two wingtip-mounted
Borstel RG-9 pivoting
laser cannons
• Two forward-facing
Dymek HM-6 concussion
missile launchers

Key Features:
• Broad-spectrum
signal jammers
• Adjustable stabilizers
for atmospheric flight
• Simple but effective
miniature hyperdrive

Its sleek arrowhead shape and enormous twin engines correctly suggest the A-wing is built for speed. It is the fastest of the Galactic Civil War-era starfighters, even outmatching the speedy TIE interceptor in straight-line acceleration and leaving such classics as X-wings and Y-wings in the space dust. A-wings give up armor and firepower for such record-breaking velocity, making it well suited for a swift strike vehicle that hits and runs in a flash. The A-wing proved so popular in the Rebellion that the model continued to be improved, and later-generation A-wings—the RZ-2—flew for the Resistance against the First Order.

FULL CIRCLE FOR
C-3PO

During the original casting for the first *Star Wars*, Anthony Daniels was won over to play the part of C-3PO by a piece of concept art by Ralph McQuarrie of the droids stranded in the desert. The painting featured an early version of C-3PO front and center and evoked a soulful sense of loneliness in an exotic environment. The artwork had a massive stone bluff in the background, a type of geography ultimately not found in the Tunisian photography for *A New Hope*. For *The Rise of Skywalker*, however, the Wadi Rum desert of Jordan perfectly matched this environment, essentially creating a moment for Daniels of stepping into his very first glimpse of C-3PO.

DOWN UNDER BOUND

Episode II was the first *Star Wars* production to shoot primarily in Australia. Whereas other productions were based in Great Britain, Episode II landed in Fox Studios Sydney. The crew included many Australian department heads and behind-the-scenes talent, as well as many Australian and New Zealand actors who were cast in major roles. In this manner, the production's location shaped the look and sound of the clone troopers of the Republic who carried actor Temuera Morrison's Maori countenance and Kiwi accent.

WHOA, MYNOCKS!

The leathery-winged pests that infest the gullet of a space slug, and end up affixing themselves to the *Millennium Falcon* in *The Empire Strikes Back*, are heard more than they're seen. They get relatively little screen time and are often obscured in the shadows. But our heroes hear them and are appropriately creeped out by their screeches. Sound designer Ben Burtt combined the sound of a horse whinny, played back at half-speed, blended with itself and appended with a seal bark to create the unique cry.

A NEW HIPPO

As part of their 2002 Episode II promotion, Ferrero of Germany, part of a worldwide candy company, used their trademarked Happy Hippo characters and cosplayed them as *Star Wars* heroes and villains. These characters—including Luke Eiwalker, Prinzessin Hippeia, Happy Han, Aubacca, Obi-Wan Hippobi, H-IPO, Erzwo Hippo, Jango Jett, and Dark Laser—would be blind-packed into chocolate Kinder eggs.

CRAIT

Galactic Placement:
Outer Rim Territories

Star:
Crait, a yellow star
Orbital Placement:
First planet from the sun

Terrain:
Salt flats; crystalline canyons;
mountain chains

Size:
7,400 kilometers in diameter

Moons:
0

Length of Day:
27 standard hours

Length of Year:
467 local days

What to Bring:
• Goggles; the bright sun
reflected off the salt flat makes
for intense midday glare.

What Happened Here?
• The Resistance fled
here and hunkered down
in an old rebel base.
• The Resistance is nearly
destroyed by Kylo Ren,
but the projected form of
Luke Skywalker distracts him.
• Rey fully opens herself up
to the Force.

AFFORDABLE
BOUNTY HUNTERS

Costume designer John Mollo had to bring in the rest of the bounty hunters for a modest budget—around $1,000 each. Not surprisingly, the posse of predators that accompany Fett on the Star Destroyer bridge are the byproduct of frugal recycling. Bossk is a repainted reptilian mask from the cantina worn on a Windak pressure suit worn by a different cantina denizen. Dengar is wearing mostly repainted stormtrooper and snowtrooper armor. Zuckuss has a newly sculpted head with bubble wrap for eyes. 4-LOM is a new head atop a repainted C-3PO body. Although IG-88 is more prop than costume, he's really a stack of spare parts. His head is part of a Rolls-Royce Derwent jet engine, previously seen behind the bar at the cantina.

ACROSS THE STARS

The biggest new piece of music added to the *Star Wars* library by composer John Williams for Episode II was the love theme between Padmé and Anakin, titled "Across the Stars." It needed to underscore the love story central to the movie which, in its rough cut, was temp-tracked in with the theme from 1970's *Love Story* by Francis Lai. Williams began recording the score with the London Symphony Orchestra in January 2002 at Abbey Road Studios. The "Across the Stars" piece was released as a single—complete with music video—on April 23, 2002.

ANAKIN SKYWALKER'S TIMELINE

- **Born** to Shmi Skywalker and—mysteriously—no father. Some speculate this indicates he is the Chosen One of ancient prophecy.

- **Age 9:** Wins the Boonta Eve Classic podrace as the only human ever to compete in such an event.

- **Age 9:** Freed from slavery by Qui-Gon Jinn and brought to the Jedi Temple on Coruscant to begin training.

- **Age 19:** Tasked with protecting Senator Padmé Amidala from would-be assassins; the two fall in love and secretly marry.

- **Age 19:** Promoted to Jedi Knight as the Clone Wars begins; takes on a Padawan, Ahsoka Tano.

- **Age 22:** Learns that his wife is pregnant and fears for her safety; makes a pact with Darth Sidious to protect her.

- **Age 22:** Anakin becomes Darth Vader and leads an assault on the Jedi Temple.

- **Age 22:** Is severely wounded by Obi-Wan Kenobi in a duel on Mustafar and cybernetically rebuilt to survive.

- **Age 41:** Hunts down the stolen Death Star plans and seeks the hidden rebel base. Duels and defeats Obi-Wan.

- **Age 44:** After discovering Luke Skywalker is his son, he tries to lure him to the dark side.

- **Age 45:** Betrays and destroys the Emperor rather than see his son suffer; dies in the light as Anakin Skywalker.

SKETCHING THE SITH

Assigned to develop a new Sith villain for *Attack of the Clones*, concept artist Dermot Power drew from his own youthful interest in martial arts to create a vampiric, samurai-like female character. "I deliberately curved the Sith's lightsaber," Power says. "I wanted something exotic, almost Arabic." Power's sketches were temporarily shelved when the veteran actor Christopher Lee signed on to play Count Dooku, but the art was later utilized for Asajj Ventress, Dooku's deadly lightsaber-wielding protégé in *The Clone Wars* animated series.

MAY THE PORSCHE BE WITH YOU

Porsche AG partnered with Lucasfilm as part of a promotion tying into the release of *The Rise of Skywalker*. This collaboration centered on designing a *Star Wars* starship, bridging the world of automotive design and a faraway galaxy's aesthetic. The finished ship, a Tri-wing S-91X Pegasus starfighter, derives its designation from the city of origin (S being Stuttgart), previous Porsche models (the 911 and 99x), and Episode IX ("1X").

WINGED WARSHIP

Technical Name:
Sienar-Jaemus Fleet Systems
Upsilon-class shuttle

You Know it As:
Kylo Ren's command shuttle

Size Specs:
37.2 meters tall with wings
folded up; 19.1 meters long;
13.5 meters wide

Weaponry:
Two twin heavy laser cannons

Key Features:
• Long-range sensor and
communications array
• Densely armored hull
• Advanced hyperdrive systems

Like a carrion bird, Kylo Ren's command shuttle circles the carnage of a battlefield, waiting to land. Upon its descent, its prodigious wings retract and fold into vertical configuration, as its landing gear and entry ramp deploy. Though Ren is a capable pilot, the shuttle is too slow and cumbersome for his impulses, and he defers to a pilot to operate it.

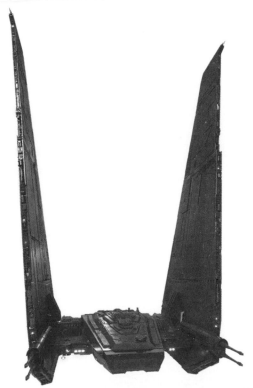

THE ILLUSTRATED CLONE WARS

In April of 2002, the starting point for Episode III before a script was ever written was to envisage the scope of the Clone Wars across seven new and distinct planets. The historic conflict would essentially be skipped as events that happened between Episodes II and III, but Lucas wanted to showcase the breadth of the war with, perhaps, an opening montage. He tasked his art department with developing these places, which included a crystal planet, a ring planet, a bridge planet, a sinkhole planet, a reef planet, and more. The art generated by this exploration instead became the backdrop for the memorable Order 66 sequence.

ROLLING OUT DROIDS

The destroyer droids started off with designs of bulky battle droids that did not transform into wheel modes but continued exploration at the concept phase, which produced that signature gimmick of the soon-to-be-nicknamed wheel droids. The tripodal legs inspired and challenged the animators required to move these machines about. "There's a good reason why there aren't any three-legged animals because it just doesn't make sense," said ILM animator Hal Hickel, who had to cheat the walk cycle of the droideka slightly. "There's a moment when the back leg has to move forward that it's just not really balanced anymore." The sound of the droidekas tumbling down the Trade Federation battleship hallways are skateboards cruising down the hallways of Sir Francis Drake High School in San Anselmo.

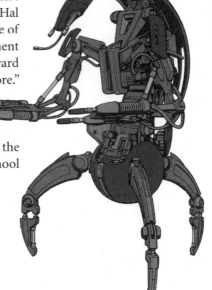

FOREST MOON OF ENDOR

Galactic Placement:
Outer Rim Territories

Star:
Ibleam, a yellow star

Orbital Placement:
The moon orbits the first planet in the system

Terrain:
Forest, plains, mountains

Size:
4,900 kilometers

Moons:
Endor is one of 9 moons

Length of Day:
18 standard hours

Length of Year:
402 local days

What to Bring:
• A power generator; Endor is primitive with no modern cities or technology. If you want to run your devices, you better power up.
• Insect repellent. Especially if you head near the swamps and don't want to end up as bugbitten as a Dulok.

What Happened Here?
• The second Death Star was under construction (and destroyed) in orbit overhead.
• Luke Skywalker reveals their parentage to Leia Organa.
• The Ewoks join the fight and help defeat the Empire.
• Darth Vader's armor is burned at a funeral pyre.

A MAZ BY ANY OTHER NAME

One of the additions J.J. Abrams supplied to the evolving story was the character of Maz Kanata, who was named Rose during development. The placeholder name and the character itself derive from Rose Gilbert, an honors English teacher in Los Angeles who had taught both Abrams and production designer Rick Carter. Gilbert, a petite older woman with a friendly wisdom and large glasses, would become the template for Maz.

ANIMATIC
ARTISTS

During the production of Episode I, the official *Star Wars* website ran a profile on Kevin Baillie and Ryan Tudhope, animatics artists working on Episode I. To inspire *Star Wars* fans looking for a future in filmmaking, the profiles made a point to mention Kevin and Ryan's ages—they were just eighteen in 1997 when they started working at Lucasfilm. Today, both are referred to as VFX veterans, supervising work at their own studio, with credits such as *Star Trek Beyond*, *Welcome to Marwen*, *Flight*, *Deadpool*, and *Ad Astra*.

HOLDO
COUTURE

Although Vice Admiral Holdo was written as the traditional hard-as-nails no-nonsense military leader, Rian Johnson switched things up by dressing Laura Dern in finery better suited to the Galactic Senate rather than the bridge of a warship. "He used the word 'balletic,'" recalls costume designer Michael Kaplan. "He wanted to see her body language. He wanted her to look a little flirtatious in some scenes with Poe, yet he wanted her to look dignified." Holdo's look is completed with a headpiece that resembles a "halo," another cue that Poe can find little traction in arguing with her.

KYLO'S NEW RIDE

Technical Name:
Sienar-Jaemus Fleet Systems customized TIE/wi interceptor

You Know it As:
Kylo Ren's TIE whisper

Size Specs:
4.1 meters tall; 15.9 meters long; 6.4 meters wide

Weaponry:
- Four wingtip ranging lasers
- Two wing bracket heavy laser cannons
- Four wing bracket medium laser cannons
- Two "chin"-mounted laser cannons
- Underslung heavy weapons turret

Key Features:
- Extended solar gather panel for maneuverability
- Hyperspace tracking sensor modules
- Hyperdrive

The TIE whisper is the latest generation of First Order TIE fighter, an upgrade of the standard TIE/fo. Improvement in hyperdrive efficiencies and miniaturization of technology have allowed lightspeed engines to be standard on this model, and the sensor brackets that frame the cockpit ball are equipped with tracking components that follow ships attempting to escape into hyperspace. Kylo Ren further modified his fighter, adding more firepower and speed to an already impressive design.

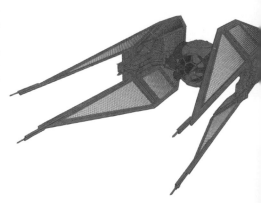

(NO) LOCATION, LOCATION, LOCATION

Although the end credits to *Revenge of the Sith* boasts filming locations like Guilin, China; Mt. Etna, Italy; Grindewald, Switzerland; Phuket, Thailand; and Tozeur, Tunisia, no first-unit crews or actors ever visited these locales for the production. Instead, small camera crews gathered footage of these places to become digital backdrops for live-action elements filmed against blue- or greenscreen. China and Thailand became Kashyyyk; Switzerland was Alderaan; Italy's Mt. Etna became lava spews on Mustafar; and Tunisia returned as Tatooine. The actors were shot against bluescreen mostly at Fox Studios Sydney, Shepperton and Elstree studios outside London, or at Industrial Light & Magic in California.

IMAGINATION OF A JEDI

"I spent a lot of time when I was a kid fighting imaginary things in my room, so when George [Lucas] puts you in that big empty green room and says you're being attacked by lots of droids, you just go in there and fight as many of them as you can. The wonderful thing is, when you go and actually see the film itself, it's amazing!"
—Samuel L. Jackson (Mace Windu)

TRAILBLAZING
WITH YOUNG INDY

In many ways, George Lucas's TV series *The Young Indiana Jones Chronicles* was a testbed for the cutting-edge digital filmmaking and production techniques he wished to make standard on the prequel trilogy. The TV show extended its budget through such digital matte paintings and crowd duplication and used now-common editorial tools to piece together disparate footage into composite takes. It's no surprise that many of the key roles from that series continued onto Episode I, including producer Rick McCallum, cinematographer David Tattersall, production designer Gavin Bocquet, set decorator Peter Walpole, and costume designer Trisha Biggar.

SURPRISE
STAR WARS CONCERT

In the lead-up to *The Force Awakens*, that there would be a big panel at 2015's San Diego Comic-Con International did not come as a surprise. What did come as a surprise is how J.J. Abrams ended said panel. The 6,000 guests in attendance were led out of Hall H to the nearby Embarcadero Marina for a *Star Wars* concert conducted by John Williams, attended by Kathleen Kennedy, Mark Hamill, Harrison Ford, and Carrie Fisher—truly a once-in-a-lifetime event. Also surprised was filmmaker Kevin Smith, who hosted the panel immediately after the *Star Wars* panel and found that the entire hall had vacated.

AT THE
STARTING LINE

The earliest incarnations of *Star Wars* were
not set "a long time ago, in a galaxy far,
far away." George Lucas's May 1973 story
treatment is set in "the 33rd century, a
period of civil wars in the galaxy." The now
familiar establishing text was absent from
the cut of the film that Marvel Comics
writer Roy Thomas saw, so the very first
issue of the *Star Wars* comics adaptation
says, "This story has no relationship to
Earth time and space. It occurs in other
solar systems in another galaxy and
could be happening in the future, the
past, or even the present." The movie's
novelization similarly was vague, stating
simply the book took place in "another
galaxy, another time."

POPULATING PORGS

Skellig Michael, the island that served as the filming location for Ahch-To, was populated with puffins that would invariably find their way into shots as they flew by. Rian Johnson was inspired to create his own feathered denizens of the island: the porgs. Concept designer Jake Lunt Davies sketched out the look of the porgs, and creature effects supervisor Neal Scanlan and his team constructed 30 porgs of various detail and performance capabilities. Each porg had about 15,000 hand-punched feathers. Some were articulated puppets, while background ones were radio controlled units that would swivel their heads and open their mouths. ILM supplemented these porgs with CG ones for performances the puppets couldn't achieve.

CASTING
ANAKIN SKYWALKER

To fill the role of the young Anakin Skywalker for Episode II, casting director Robin Gurland received more than 1,500 submissions and viewed more than 400 videotaped auditions before narrowing down the list of candidates to thirty to bring to George Lucas's approval. Of those thirty, Lucas wittled the list down to five. In the first week of May 2000, just seven weeks before production was to start, these five were given a screen test opposite Natalie Portman at Skywalker Ranch. A young Canadian actor named Hayden Christensen won the role of a lifetime.

KNUCKLE DRAGGER

Technical Name:
Kuat-Entralla Drive Yards
All Terrain MegaCaliber
Six transport

You Know it As:
AT-M6 walker

Size Specs:
40.9 meters long; 36.2 meters
tall; 18 meters wide

Weaponry:
- One MegaCaliber Six
turbolaser cannon
- Two heavy fire-linked
laser cannons
- Two medium anti-ship
laser cannons

Key Features:
- Turbolaser power cells
- Oversize forelegs brace
against turbolaser recoil

The largest of the First Order walkers, the AT-M6 is a terrifying, gorilla-like war machine with a prime weapon capable of punching through shielded armor. The walker's powerful limbs are reinforced and can tear through the tow cables that once brought down the AT-AT walkers of the previous generation.

UTAPAU
AT LAST

In the earliest drafts of the original
Star Wars, the planet we now know as
Tatooine was called Utapau. At the start
of the development of *The Phantom
Menace*, Naboo was, for a time, called
Utapau. *Revenge of the Sith* would be the
movie where the name, that had been
kicking around George Lucas's notebook
and draft scripts for decades, would finally
find a home. The "sinkhole planet" design
developed for Episode III was informed
by early Joe Johnston sketches of the
"crevasse city" of Sicemon for *Return of
the Jedi* and a Ralph McQuarrie piece of a
canyon city on Alderaan done in 1993 for
The Illustrated Star Wars Universe book.

THE RISE OF KENNER

In the mid-1970s, Mego Toys was the big player in action figures. However, the company went defunct in 1983—if only it hadn't rejected the right to make *Star Wars* toys. At the time, they didn't see much commercial value in the movie when it was approached by *Star Wars* producers in 1976. Instead, the makers of *Star Wars* signed up the relatively small toy company Kenner to produce items based on the movie. It would eventually make Kenner one of the biggest toy companies in the world. In 1991, Kenner was purchased by Hasbro.

FLYING THE *FALCON*

For the first time in a *Star Wars* movie, the *Millennium Falcon*'s cockpit could soar. In previous films, the cockpit set could be rattled and rocked by off-camera stagehands, but the real sense of motion was pantomined by the actors aboard. For *The Force Awakens*, audiences would really feel the G's pulled by Rey in her daring escape from Jakku because they were real. Special effects supervisor Chris Corbould and his crew mounted the cockpit on a hydraulic six-axis gimbal at Pinewood Studios. With this rig, the effects crew could rotate the cockpit 360 degrees and tilt 30 degrees on any axis. "That created great shadow interactions and reactions from the actors," Corbould said.

PADME AMIDALA'S TIMELINE

Born on Naboo to Ruwee and Jobal Naberrie; has older sister Sola Naberrie.

Age 12: Joins the Legislative Youth Program; has a young crush on an artist named Palo.

Age 14: Elected monarch of Naboo. Is embroiled in the blockade of the planet.

Age 14: Liberates Naboo with the help of the Jedi, the Gungans, and Anakin Skywalker; instrumental to Senator Palpatine's ascent to Chancellor.

Age 24: While serving as Senator of Naboo, is targeted for assassination by Nute Gunray of the Trade Federation.

Age 24: Palpatine assigns Anakin Skywalker to serve as Padmé's bodyguard; Amidala and Skywalker start to fall in love.

Age 24: As the Clone Wars erupt, Anakin and Padmé secretly wed on Naboo.

Age 24: Throughout the Clone Wars, Padmé seeks diplomatic solution to end the war while her husband goes to fight on the frontlines of the growing conflict.

Age 27: Padmé is pregnant; Anakin fears for her safety. He turns to the dark side seeking power to protect her.

Age 27: On Polis Massa, Padmé dies giving birth to twins, Luke and Leia.

HANDY HOMAGES
IN MARVEL'S PHASE 2

As producer Kevin Feige was developing and producing Phase 2 of the Marvel Cinematic Universe slate (which ran from 2013–2015), he showed his *Star Wars* fan roots by sneaking in an homage to *The Empire Strikes Back*. In every Phase 2 film (*Iron Man 3*, *Thor: The Dark World*, *Captain America: The Winter Soldier*, *Guardians of the Galaxy*, *Avengers: Age of Ultron*, and *Ant-Man*), somebody gets a hand or arm cut off.

CANTO BIGHT
INSPIRATION

The Canto Bight sequence began as an extended homage to Alfred Hitchcock's 1955 classic *To Catch a Thief*. The opulent French Riviera is the setting for the film and centers around a jewel thief preying on the rich tourists about. In an early draft of Rian Johnson's screenplay for *The Last Jedi*, Finn and Rose would find the Master Codebreaker and accompany him on a rooftop heist that mirrored a moment in the earlier film.

CASTING REY

Rey's interrogation by Kylo Ren was the scene Daisy Ridley read on her audition that landed her the role. "She just blew my mind," director J.J. Abrams said of Ridley's performance. "She was just so emotional. She was spot-on." There is much going on in the subtext of the sequence, not the least of which is the creeping realization that the door that Kylo has opened into Rey's mind swings both ways. In trying to peer into Rey's secrets, Kylo has revealed his own fears to her, as well as a hint of what mind tricks are possible with the Force.

NABOO

Galactic Placement:
Mid Rim Territories
Star: Naboo, a yellow star

Orbital Placement:
Third planet from the sun

Terrain:
Forest, grassland
plains, lakes, swamps

Size:
12,120 kilometers in diameter

Moons:
3

Length of Day:
26 standard hours

Length of Year:
312 local days

What to Bring:
• Spare luggage; Naboo artisans
are renowned the galaxy over for
their craft, and you'll want to
bring home some souvenirs.
• Swimming trunks; clear, freshwater lakes
dot Naboo's entire surface.

What Happened Here?
• A Trade Federation blockade
allows for Senator Palpatine to be
elected Supreme Chancellor.
• Qui-Gon Jinn is killed by Darth Maul.
• Obi-Wan Kenobi defeats
Maul—or does he?
• Padmé Amidala and Anakin Skywalker
fall in love and secretly marry.

THE HIDDEN 1138

Star Wars fans know to scour the movies for certain "Easter eggs," hidden references to other Lucasfilm productions. One of the most pervasive is a reference to *THX 1138*, George Lucas's first feature film. In *Star Wars*, Luke mentions it as a cell-block number on the Death Star. In *Empire*, it's tucked into an order to send snowspeeders Rogues 10 and 11 to station 3-8. But the *Jedi* one went unspotted for years. It was assumed to be nonexistent. It was not until a close look at the Boushh costume in anticipation of making a high-end collectible in the 2000s did a keen-eyed Lucasfilm staffer spot it: the number "1138" is painted on the right side of Boushh's helmet.

JUNKING
A JUNK
PLANET
CONNECTION

The Force Awakens and the animated series *Star Wars Rebels* were both in concurrent development, and early on there was some idea of connecting the two via a shared setting. It was known that Episode VII would feature a "Junk Planet" with shipwrecks of classic trilogy vehicles. *Rebels* would be set in a world destined to become an Imperial factory. Could they be one in the same? The shifting schedules of development and the needs of an animated series versus live-action location work would junk this idea. The plan fell by the wayside, and Lothal and Jakku developed on divergent paths.

THE GALAXY TO THE RESCUE

The enormous space battle that ends *The Rise of Skywalker* required every available era-appropriate flying craft ILM could muster to fill the skies over Exegol. This included pulling from non-film sources—starships that had previously flown in the various Lucasfilm animated series. From *The Clone Wars* came Mandalorian gauntlet fighters, T-6 shuttles, Zygerrian freighters, and Lantillian haulers. From *Star Wars Rebels* come the *Ghost*, Wookiee gunships, Lancer pursuit ships, and a YT-2400 freighter. From *Star Wars Resistance* come Jarek Yeager, Torra Doza, and Kazudo Xiono in their racers. And zipping in from Star Tours is the Starspeeder 1000! In total, the reinforcements numbered 14,448 ships.

SITH
SPORTSMANSHIP

Composer John Williams utilized a music technique called a *leitmotif*, which is a recurring theme assigned to a specific character and used intermittently throughout a work. Darth Vader's theme, "The Imperial March," is now a favorite of college marching bands in football stadiums everywhere. Williams explains this phenomenon by noting that the music is "military in an ominous and aggressive sense… That's probably why they use it."

SKIMMING THE SURFACE

Technical Name:
Roche Machines modified V-4X-D

You Know it As:
Resistance ski speeders

Size Specs:
7.3 meters long; 11.5 meters wide; 4.3 meters tall

Weaponry:
- Two medium laser cannons

Key Features:
- Open-air cockpit
- Halofoil mono-ski for stability
- Advanced navigation sensors

The Resistance ski speeders are actually old Rebel Alliance surplus found left behind at the Crait outpost. These, in turn, were lightweight recreational vehicles that the rebels reinforced and equipped with weaponry. They are low-altitude repulsorcraft that rely on a mono-ski for terrain stabilization, leaving a carved trail in their wake.

MOVIE CAMP

As Rian Johnson began story development on *The Last Jedi*, he invited development executives at Lucasfilm as well as concept artists to join him in a series of screenings wherein he hoped to communicate some of the themes, tones, and textures he hoped to explore in his film. Among the films seen were *Letter Never Sent*, *Three Outlaw Samurai*, *Twelve O'Clock High*, *The Bridge on the River Kwai*, and *Gunga Din*.

SILLY NAMES FOR FEARSOME CREATURES

Most of the creatures lurking in the background of Jabba's palace would never have their names spoken aloud, but they all had some sort of moniker. Some of these would be exposed to *Star Wars* fans through action figures or trading cards, often revealing the playful or punchdrunk nature of the overworked ILM Creature Shop when they named these oddballs. Salacious B. Crumb's name started off from a misspoken utterance of "shoelaces" as "Soolacious"; Ephant Mon takes clear inspiration from "Elephant Man." The mole-like Elom just need to look at his name a mirror to find the source of his handle. Ree-Yees was "Three Eyes," and Hermi Odle's silly name ("Hear Me Yodel") is an improvement over his first name, Hemmy Moroid.

LONELY ON DAGOBAH

"I was the only human being on the call sheet for months," said Mark Hamill of the challenge of filming the Dagobah sequences for *The Empire Strikes Back*. With Kenny Baker tucked inside his R2-D2 shell, and Frank Oz and his puppeteering assistants concealed below the stage, Hamill not only had to play his part but compensate for not being able to hear Yoda's dialogue. Director Irvin Kershner credited Hamill for making Yoda work because the audience believes Luke is interacting with a living being, and his performance brings Yoda alive.

RECORD-BREAKING MODEL WORK

Although often correctly lauded for its breakthroughs in computer-generated visual effects, *The Phantom Menace* also boasts some of the most elaborate and complex modelmaking and miniature photography work in Industrial Light & Magic's history. "More models were built for Episode I than in the entirety of the original trilogy of Episodes IV, V, and VI," said Steve Gawley, ILM model shop supervisor for Episode I. "In total, we built 500-plus models, miniature sets, and characters for this show. We employed as many as eighty-seven modelmakers at a time, with an average of sixty for a full year. It was huge."

A GALACTIC TOYBOX

George Lucas dismisses the notion that licensing and merchandising was always part of his grand plan. "It certainly wasn't something anybody predicted, especially us," he says. "The first toys didn't come out until a year after the first film came out, and it's grown into this big opportunity, which has helped finance the movies for me. I enjoy toys, and I make the films to stimulate the imaginations of the audience and especially the young people who see the film."

OUT OF
HIBERNATION

During the earliest story meetings regarding *The Last Jedi*, the movie *Legends of the Fall* came up as a narrative touchpoint in reference to Luke, particularly the grizzly bear that appears at the end. From that, Rian Johnson began jokingly calling the movie Space Bear, which stuck as its code name. Not only did the name stick, but it carried through to all the code names used in film documentation. Luke Skywalker was Space Bear, Rey was Goldilocks, Finn was Ted, Poe was Smokey, Phasma was Panda, Rose was Koala, Kylo was Grizzly, BB-8 was Booboo, and Snoke (Pooh)'s Star Destroyer was the "Hundred Acre Wood."

WHAT'S MY MOTIVATION?

When shooting the confrontation between Jango Fett and Obi-Wan Kenobi in the Fett apartment on Kamino on July 26, 2000, Ewan McGregor had an acting note to pass along to 13-year-old Daniel Logan, who was playing the 10-year-old Boba Fett. Boba was supposed to look at Obi-Wan with a look of suspicion bordering on disgust. Logan may have overdone it, thanks to McGregor's note. "Ewan told me to look at him as if he'd let off a really smelly fart!" George Lucas's direction? "Okay, but a little less smelly this time."

KYLO REN'S TIMELINE

Born on Chandrila as Ben Solo to Leia Organa and Han Solo. From an early age would show an affinity for the Force.

Age 10: Luke Skywalker begins training Ben in the ways of the Jedi, truly awakening him to the Force. At this time, Rey is born far, far away.

Age 23: Already groomed toward the dark side by mysterious voices, Ben snaps and attacks Luke and burns his Jedi temple.

Age 23: Having seemingly committed to darkness, Ben goes to Snoke and then seeks out the Knights of Ren.

Age 23: After defeating the leader of the Knights of Ren, assumes that mantle and renames himself Kylo Ren.

Age 29: On a search for Luke Skywalker, tangles with the Resistance, meets Rey, and kills Han Solo.

Age 29: Forges a powerful Force connection with Rey.

Age 29: Kills Snoke, becomes Supreme Leader of the First Order.

Age 30: Drawn to the mysterious world of Exegol, he seeks out answers regarding the mystery of the resurrected Emperor.

Age 30: Compelled by his mother's sacrifice and memories of his father, Kylo Ren rejects the dark side, returning as Ben Solo to help Rey in her attempt to stop the resurrected Emperor. He dies restoring her life through their shared power as a dyad in the Force.

WICKET
STEPS UP

Kenny Baker, veteran performer who had played R2-D2 in the original trilogy, was originally slated to play Wicket, the Ewok who befriends Princess Leia in the Endor forest. A bout of food poisoning took him out of action and opened the way for 11-year-old Warwick Davis to become a star. Davis had impressed the filmmakers with his energy and life he brought to his Ewok character—so much so that his character was rechristened Wicket W. Warrick. Baker would get his moment to shine, though. His character was renamed Paploo and is the Ewok who bravely (or foolishly, depending on your point of view) steals the Imperial speeder bike.

ISN'T THAT SPECIAL?

Technical Name:
Sienar-Jaemus Fleet Systems TIE/sf space superiority starfighter

You Know it As:
Special Forces TIE fighter

Size Specs:
6.7 meters tall long

Weaponry:
Two forward SJFS L-s9.6 laser cannons; underslung SJFS Lb-14 heavy weapons turret; KDY Arakyd ST7 concussion and mag-pulse warhead launcher

Key Features:
Tandem ejection seats; extended range deuterium tanks; miniaturized hyperdrive

There are worse vehicles you can steal if you're thinking of defecting from the First Order. The TIE/sf fighter is a marked improvement over the classic TIE fighter designs once found in the Galactic Empire ranks. A hyperdrive means the ship is not dependent on a carrier craft for extrasystem travel. Shields and armor make it tougher than the fragile TIEs, and a rear gunner means it is more than capable of discouraging enemy pursuit.

LUKE SKYWALKER'S DESTINY

Years before *The Last Jedi* began development, the treatment left behind by George Lucas in 2012 also had Episode VIII be the one wherein Luke Skywalker would die.

DREAMING UP A
DROID FACTORY

Demonstrating the flexibility afforded by digital cinema, George Lucas envisioned a major action sequence months after principal photography had wrapped. In March of 2001, after editing the movie and finding the need to replace talky exposition scenes with fast-paced action, Lucas returned to the set, this time in Ealing Studios in London, and shot live-action elements of Hayden Christensen (Anakin) and Natlie Portman (Padmé) against bluescreen. ILM then built the elaborate droid factory around them. Animators closely studied reference photography of automated car factories to capture the feel of heavy machinery moving quickly. The foundation of the factory—the far wall and several pillars—were practical models, but all the moving machinery, droid parts, and Geonosian workers were computer-generated.

BB-BEEPS

Ben Burtt, Matthew Wood, and David Acord collaborated with actors Ben Schwartz and Bill Hader to give BB-8 a distinct voice. Schwartz vocalized a temporary performance with the emphasis being on emotion, to understand his particular state in scenes, as well as to give something for performers on set (like Daisy Ridley) to react to. With this layer of performance, Skywalker Sound crafted a range of sounds that were then fed to Bill Hader via a device called a talk box, who manipulated them into a performance.

YODA
IN WAITING

As Episode III entered post-production, ILM Animation Supervisor Rob Coleman was eager to get started on refining Yoda, adding new improvements to the CG model including more realistic translucency to the skin and the little "pilling" of fabric that happens on his robe. Unfortunately, none of the Yoda shots were ready to be turned over to work just yet. He did not want to lose his crack team of animators to another production, so he proposed an alternate project to get them started on Yoda—replacing the puppet incarnation from Episode I with the new Episode II model. This animation work started in 2003 yet would not be seen by the public until released in Blu-ray format in 2011.

CRITICAL RECEPTION

George Lucas famously did not pay much heed to critics and stood behind his work regardless of professional reception. During the production of Episode I, Lucas could be spotted wearing a T-shirt with a review of *Star Wars* on it. A closer inspection revealed it was more than met the eye: the text is from a *New Yorker* story about the film's 20th anniversary and reads: "*STAR WARS*...a film with comic-book characters, unbelievable story, no political or social commentary, lousy acting, preposterous dialogue, and a ridiculously simplistic morality. In other words, a BAD MOVIE."

HOTH

Galactic Placement:
Outer Rim Territories
Star: Hoth, a blue-white star

Orbital Placement:
Sixth planet in the system

Terrain:
Snow and ice

Size:
7,200 kilometers

Moons:
3

Length of Day:
23 standard hours

Length of Year:
549 local days

What to Bring:
• Bundle up! Temperatures routinely drop below -40 degrees standard; exposed skin can freeze solid in seconds
• A portable shelter. No matter how well you dress, a Hoth nighttime blizzard will cut through the warmest furs. Best to hunker down in place and let the snow insulate you until the sun rises.

What Happened Here?
• Luke Skywalker first saw an image of a spectral Obi-Wan telling him to go to Dagobah.
• The Empire strikes back in a major ground assault and wins a key victory.

WHEN IT RAINS, AGAIN...

During principal photography, a ferocious thunderstorm tore apart the Episode I set in Tozeur, Tunisia, on July 29, 1997. The Podrace Arena and Mos Espa sets were battered, dressing room tents were ripped apart, and props and costumes were taken by the winds. Producer Rick McCallum hastily rearranged the schedule to not lose time as they rebuilt. George Lucas serenely took the incident as an indicator of good luck, given that the same thing happened on the first *Star Wars* movie.

PRICING THE DEATH STAR

While budgeting the visual effects of *Return of the Jedi*, some of the financial advisors wanted to talk George Lucas out of realizing the second Death Star as a miniature, relying instead on more affordable matte paintings. ILM Model Shop supervisor Lorne Peterson was advised not to bring up the subject of the Death Star's cost in dollars, though he did feel the model was the right way to go for the types of shots the movie required. Peterson—as requested—did not mention the price, but he did know that Lucas had recently purchased a 1962 Dino Ferrari in need of restoration work. So, Peterson told Lucas that a model of the second Death Star would cost "just a bit more than the Ferrari that you bought." Lucas agreed, and the budget-minded producers couldn't object to an unknown number.

THE RHYTHM OF
REY AND REN

The key new themes composed by John Williams for *The Force Awakens* were those for Rey and Kylo Ren. "Rey for me was particularly difficult," Willaims said. "It's kind of an adventure theme in a way. She's a girl who's been a scavenger, who's been alone, she's without her parents. I felt a lot of empathy for this poor creature who's at once brilliant and can defend herself... But you want to touch something in her that's vulnerable and recognizes her need." For Kylo, Williams deliberately evoked his work with Darth Vader. "If it can convey in a few short notes the way the "Imperial March" does evil power, it will need to be something that will hit you and is accessible right away."

YOU SEEK
TOYOTA

To promote the release of *A New Hope* in 1977, 20th Century Fox gave away a customized Toyota Celica. The vehicle was emblazoned with decals of characters from the film. No record of who won the car can be found at the offices of Lucasfilm, and they lost track of it entirely in the late 1980s. According to one source, it was listed around that time in a toy collector's magazine with a meager $1,000 asking price. Since it's truly "one of a kind," the car could sell for somewhere in the six figures.

THE CROSSGUARD SABER

Technical Name:
Not applicable; this is a handcrafted item

You Know it As:
Kylo Ren's lightsaber

Size Specs:
29.8 centimeter hilt length; 14 centimeter hilt width

When It Was Made:
After Ben Solo joined the Knights of Ren

Key Features:
• A cracked kyber crystal producing an unstable weapon
• Ragged blade
• Quillon emitters

Who It's Killed (a partial list):
• Lor San Tekka
• Han Solo
• Several Praetorian Guards
• Boolio

Intense and volatile, Kylo Ren's blade mirrors the man himself. Built on the body of his original Jedi lightsaber, Kylo has modified it by overpowering its crystal. The cracked power source now requires excess energy venting to keep the unstable weapon from exploding. These vents become the quillon blades, two smaller blades that stick out perpendicular to the hilt.

WHEN IT SNOWS...

During the first week of location shooting on *The Empire Strikes Back*, Norway was hit with an unexpected blizzard that buried the production under ten feet of snow. Stranded in their hotel, the crew shot what they could just outside the hotel entrance, including Luke Skywalker's slog through the snow after escaping the wampa ice creature's lair.

WOOKIEE WORLD

For Episode III, George Lucas would at last get to visit a proper, cinematic Kashyyyk populated by Wookiee warriors. Aside from Peter Mayhew reprising his role as Chewbacca, the Wookiees were five towering locals from Australia cast for their height, bulked out even more with padded suits and shoes, and draped in synthetic fur to become Wookiees. Despite a built-in circulatory system that pumped cool water into their suits, these performers would overheat often. Bolstering these ranks would be motion-captured computer-generated Wookiees performed by Australian basketball player Michael Kingma. "We got an XXXXL mo-cup suit," said ILM Animation Supervisor Rob Coleman. "It was a lot better than having a six-foot-tall person doing all the actions and then trying to translate that to a seven-foot-tall Wookiee."

REY'S TIMELINE

Born to parents on the run from a dark secret.

Age 6: Rey is abandoned on Jakku and sold off to Unkar Plutt by her parents to protect her from cultists of Exegol.

Age 19: Rey crosses paths with a Resistance droid, BB-8, and an ex-stormtrooper named Finn.

Age 19: Rey and Finn use the *Millennium Falcon* to escape Jakku, which attracts the attention of Han Solo and Chewbacca.

Age 19: Captured by Kylo Ren, the Force truly awakens in Rey as she is swept off in an adventure for the Resistance.

Age 19: Rey finds Luke Skywalker on Ahch-To and entreaties him to train her and return to help the Resistance.

Age 19: Rey forges a strong Force connection with Kylo and goes to him in a misguided attempt to turn him back from the dark.

Age 20: Rey continues her Jedi journey, training with Leia Organa.

Age 20: Rey and her friends undertake the vital mission of determining the secrets of the resurrected Emperor.

Age 20: Rey learns that her parents fled from Palpatine, for she was Palpatine's granddaughter. Ben and Rey join forces to defeat this undead menace.

DISARMING BOBA FETT

In the lead-up to *The Empire Strikes Back*, kids already knew of Boba Fett from his appearance on toy packaging promising him to be a breakout star of the upcoming *Star Wars* movie. In 1979, kids could have clipped proofs of purchases from action figure packaging and mailed away to get an exclusive, not-yet-available-in-stores Boba Fett action figure with missile-launching backpack. When the Fett figures arrived, kids instead found the rocket glued in place and a note stating that the feature had been removed from the figure "for safety reasons." Despite many an urban legend to the contrary, a rocket-firing Fett figure was never mailed out in this era, though prototypes of the toy have since made it to the collectors market and are incredibly rare.

BIG CITY LIVING

Some of the earliest concepts for *Return of the Jedi* set the story on the city-covered Imperial planet of Had Abbadon. The Emperor's throne room could be found deep beneath the multi-leveled city, closer to the planet's lava-streaked surface. These concepts would later inform the creation of Coruscant, the city-planet featured in the prequels. Before Had Abbadon was written out of the story, it was orbited by a "sanctuary moon," a forest moon deliberately kept clear of construction so as to remain lush and pristine. This would become the Moon of Endor.

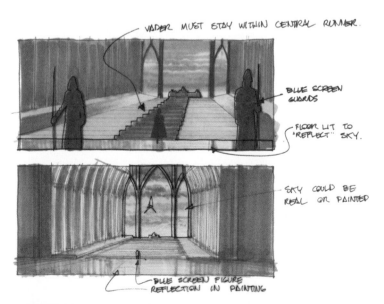

VADER MUST STAY WITHIN CENTRAL RUNNER.

BLUE SCREEN GUARDS

FLOOR LIT TO "REFLECT" SKY.

SKY COULD BE REAL OR PAINTED

BLUE SCREEN FIGURE REFLECTION IN PAINTING

AKI-AKI
APLENTY

The call for thousands (500,000, as per the script) of jubilating Aki Aki in the Forbidden Valley of Pasaana proved a daunting task for Neal Scanlan and his creature effects crew. Dividing and conquering the need was the best approach. Even with digital crowd replication, there would be upward of 500 extras assembled in the Wadi Rum desert of Jordan for the sequence. While seventy had animatronic heads with articulated trunks, the vast majority of them, seen at a distance from camera, are wearing printed fabric hoods with photography of the Aki-Aki designs on them.

FOR JEDI ON THE MOVE

Technical Name:
Kuat Systems Engineering
Aethersprite-class Delta-7

You Know it As:
Jedi starfighter

Size Specs:
8 meters long; 3.9 meters wide

Performance:
Sublight speed of 110 MGLT;
atmospheric airspeed
of 1,150 kph

Weaponry:
• Two forward-facing Taim Co.
sds 8/5 laser cannons

Key Features:
• Separate hyperspace
docking ring
• Abbreviated astromech socket
• Long-range
communications array

Before the galaxy erupted in the Clone Wars, Jedi traveled to worlds on Republic cruisers or in single-passenger Jedi starfighters like the tiny Delta-7 models. The spearhead-shaped craft is cramped and not designed for long-range travel, though it can dock with a hyperdrive ring for faster-than-light jumps. The ship is very small, making it hard for passive sensors to pinpoint. The Delta-7B model has a larger droid socket just fore of the cockpit, which allows it to carry full-size R2 units.

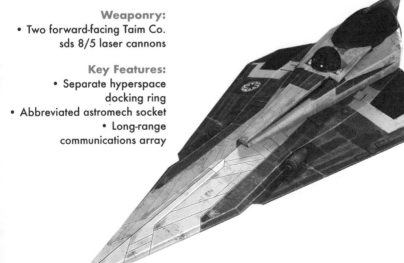

A CITY IN THE
CLOUDS

The idea of Cloud City dates back to
unused concepts for the Imperial capital
city in the original *Star Wars*. The story
would have visited Alderaan, described
in the earlier drafts as the capital of the
Galactic Empire. The gaseous world
would feature "an island city suspended in
a sea of Cirrus Methane." Budget restraints
on the first movie meant this environment
would be discarded, and the action there
was folded into the Death Star instead,
but the city-in-the-clouds concept would
return in *The Empire Strikes Back*.

MUSTAFAR
MEGA-TURE

Revenge of the Sith features one of the largest miniatures ever built for a *Star Wars* film: the volcanic planet Mustafar. Built at 1/134 scale, the twenty-foot-wide by thirty-six-foot-long set had a river of molten lava carving its way across a mountainous valley. Canted at ten degrees to create a slow-moving flow of lava, the miniature incorporated 15,000 gallons of the food-thickening agent methocel for lava, which was lit from beneath as it traveled down transparent plastic riverbeds, and crusted with a mixture that included burned cork and cat litter.

RITE OF
WOOKIEE PASSAGE

For *The Force Awakens*, Peter Mayhew—the actor behind the original Chewbacca—was able to reprise his classic role but in a limited fashion. Recovering from knee surgery meant Mayhew could not be mobile, but he did play Chewie while seated in his co-pilot's seat. More importantly, he taught the Wookiee ropes to young Joonas Suotamo, a Finnish actor and former professional basketball star who played the more mobile Chewbacca in that film. Having proved himself capable of inheriting the role, for *The Last Jedi* Suotamo played Chewbacca solo—that is, without Mayhew in the role, but certainly with his blessing.

DARTH VADER
RE-ASSEMBLED

Episode III would culminate with the re-appearance of Darth Vader in full black armor, which required a close examination of the original costumes of the first trilogy. Costume designer Trisha Biggar and costume props supervisor Ivo Coveney took stock of how much the costume changed from film to film and realized the freshly assembled look for modern audiences required revisiting the design. The original helmet had a hand-crafted, asymmetrical look which was at odds at the sleek, machine-made mask required by the story. The helmet was re-sculpted with finer detail, smoother lines, and a symmetry that was once absent. Padding and lifts accommodate the height difference between Hayden Christensen and David Prowse.

STAR WARS
ON THE RADIO

At the height of *Star Wars'* popularity in 1981, George Lucas essentially donated the rights to produce a dramatization of his film to National Public Radio. The end result is a 13-episode audio-only version of the story, written by Brian Daley and directed by John Madden, that expands the action of the film to over six hours and adds new scenes and characters. Actors Mark Hamill and Anthony Daniels reprise their film roles on radio, joined by Perry King as Han Solo, Ann Sachs as Princess Leia, and Brock Peters as Darth Vader.

HOLOCHESS REPRISE

When Finn is aboard the *Millennium Falcon* in *The Force Awakens*, he inadvertently triggers the holochess chambles, and the tiny animated beasties spring to life. Sharp-eyed viewers will note that the monsters are continuing their fight from Episode IV, as if they've been on pause since 1977. The creatures were originally animated by Phil Tippett and Jon Berg as one of the last effects created for the first *Star Wars*. To recreate the effect, J.J. Abrams wanted to return to stop-motion animation and recruited Tippett Studio to work its magic. The first challenge was tracking down the original puppets for reference. Four were found in the Lucasfilm Archives. Two were discovered to be in the personal collection of filmmaker Peter Jackson.

THE ROSE
PARADE

In 2007, George Lucas served as grand marshal of the Tournament of Roses and rang in the year of the 30th anniversary of *Star Wars* in a big way. The Parade's eco-friendly theme that year was reflected in two flower-covered floats commemorating Endor and Naboo, but these were not the showstopping elements of Lucas's presence in the parade. He had invited 200 members of the fan costuming group the 501st Legion from around the world to march as the largest assemblage of Imperial stormtroopers and accompanied them with the high-stepping Grambling State University Tiger Marching Band (also decked out in *Star Wars* costumes). The challenge of putting all this together was showcased in *Star Warriors*, a documentary produced of the event that was included in the 2011 *Star Wars* Blu-ray set.

EXEGOL

Galactic Placement:
The Unknown Regions

Star:
Exegol, a blue-white star
Orbital Placement:
First from the sun

Terrain:
Barren rock and desert flats

Size:
13,649 kilometers in diameter

Moons:
0

Length of Day:
53 standard hours

Length of Year:
210 local days

What to Bring:
• A Sith wayfinder. There's no other way to reliably travel through the cosmic bramble of the Unknown Regions without such an artifact.
• Courage. Exegol is one of the darkest, most terrifying places in the galaxy.

What Happened Here?
• The Sith Eternal cult took root here, worshipping the dark side and trying to bring about a new age of the Sith.
• Dark sciences, alchemy, and the Force have somehow resurrected Darth Sidious.
• A fleet of powerful new warships were built in secret in underground shipyards.
• The final confrontation between the galaxy and the diabolical First Order.

SKYWALKER RANCH

As a film student at the University of Southern California, George Lucas dreamed of building his own facility for postproduction sound and editing, "a big fraternity where filmmakers could work together and create together." Using the profits from both *American Graffiti* and *Star Wars*, he transformed a 1,700-acre ranch (later expanded to cover more than 6,500 acres) in Marin County, California, into Skywalker Ranch. The Victorian-styled Main House contains Lucas's offices and his research library, which greatly informed the visual and narrative development of the prequel trilogy and the films that followed.

A FATE BEST SERVED COLD

Technical Name:
Figg and Associates Class-3 CFC

You Know it As:
Carbon-freezing chamber

Size Specs:
5.5-meter diameter platform

Key Features:
- Life-form indicators
- Repulsorlift-equipped freezing block
- Liquid carbonite reservoir
- Crack technical crew of Ugnaught workers

Carbon-freezing is a way of storing volatile substance—like tibanna gas or coaxium fuel—in a stasis-like hibernation field. With modifications, a carbon-freezing chamber can freeze a living subject, encasing them in carbonite and suspended animation. Victims of carbon-freezing describe the ordeal as a "big, wide awake nothing." Upon thawing, these victims may further suffer hibernation sickness, with symptoms ranging from disorientation to temporary blindness. Carbonite can naturally occur in huge fields of deep space carbonbergs, like the swarm known to pollute the space around the Kessel Run.

GUEST DIRECTOR
IN ANIMATICS

When his friend and colleague Steven
Spielberg expressed interest in the
burgeoning field of animatics, George
Lucas invited him to play with the tools
he had developed and try his hand and
previsualizing several segments of *Revenge
of the Sith*. Spielberg and the Episode III
animatics crew created low-rez versions
of the Utapau chase, the Emperor/Yoda
duel, and the Mustafar duel, which were
audacious, action-packed, and far too big
and elaborate to fit in the movie. Pieces of
Spielberg's sequences were released on the
Star Wars Blu-ray set.

STAR WARS GETS POLITICAL/ POLITICS GET *STAR WARS*-Y

Although *Star Wars* was set in a faraway galaxy, topics such as Watergate and the Vietnam War could not help but shape its narrative, for they deeply affected the American psyche. The reverse was true in the 1980s, when the huge pop culture success of *Star Wars* began permeating political discussion, particularly the presidency of Ronald Reagan. In a March 8, 1983, speaking engagement at the National Association of Evangelicals, Reagan referred to the Soviet Union as "an evil empire," and later that same month, he proposed the space-based Strategic Defense Initiative, which would soon be dubbed "Star Wars" in beltway speak, much to Lucasfilm's chagrin.

SEEKING YODA

George Lucas killed off Obi-Wan Kenobi in the first *Star Wars* film and found himself in need of a mentor character to take Luke onto his next steps in Jedi training. The earliest iteration of what would become Yoda was a frog-like being named "Minch Yoda." Screenwriter Lawrence Kasdan helped Lucas develop Yoda's inverted speech, giving his dialogue a "medieval feeling with religious overtones." To performer Frank Oz, Yoda's peculiar syntax dates back to a more formal age.

TROPICAL
GREAT BRITAIN

As exotic and tropical as the rainforest planet of Ajan Kloss looks on screen, it is located far from the tropics. It's in Black Park, an area of greenery adjacent to Pinewood Studios outside of London. An unseasonably warm summer that stretched into September helped sell the illusion of a jungle, but it was really the digital landscaping and greenery added by Industrial Light & Magic that transplanted the action from Great Britain to a jungle moon far, far away.

THE FATHIER TRACK
STAR WARS:
EPISODE VIII THE LAST JEDI

EXT. CASINO BALCONY
Rose walks as if in a trance to one of the viewing
balconies that peer out at an enormous banked
RACE TRACK.

> FINN
> What are those things?

A race is in progress - beautifully dressed spectators
cheer as jockeys ride glorious beasts, each the size
of a large horse but with the sleek noble curves of
a great dane. Poetry in motion.

> ROSE
> Fathiers! I've never seen a real one.

> FINN
> Look, this whole place is beautiful. I mean, come
> on. Why do you hate it so much?

> ROSE
> Look closer.

Finn steps to a set of electrobinoculars built into
the balcony ledge and peers through them. He zooms
in and watches the jockeys beating the poor beasts
to make them go faster. He pans over to the see
the loathsome stablemaster whipping a fathier and
smacking the stable boy who tries to intervene.

                    ROSE (cont'd)
My sister and I grew up in a poor mining system. The
First Order stripped our ore to finance our military
then shelled us to test their weapons. They took
everything we had. And who do you think these people
are? There's only one business in the galaxy that
will get you this rich.

                    FINN
War.

                    ROSE
Selling weapons to the First Order. I wish I could
put my fist through this whole lousy beautiful town.

BB-8 rolls up to them, suspiciously rattling like a
piggy bank, beeping wildly.

_____

In Rian Johnson's development of the fathiers, he described them as alien but
horse-like and gentle in nature. He wanted a design that at first glance read as
beautiful, but upon closer examination showed a weariness and pain. Concept
artist Aaron McBride iterated hundreds of designs before cracking the look of
the majestic beasts.

THX ORIGINS

Dissatisfied with the difference in sound quality between a professional mixing studio and the average movie theater, George Lucas enlisted audio scientist Tomlinson Holman to define the standards of audio and picture quality required to preserve the optimum filmgoing experience for audiences. The end result was the THX Group within Lucasfilm, which began rolling out these standards of certifications to movie theaters across the nation. In time, these standards would apply to home systems and car audio. THX was spun off as its own company in 2002. Although THX stands for the "Tomlinson Holman Experiment," it is also a nod to George Lucas's first feature film, *THX 1138*.

FROM KING TO
PHASMA

The look of Captain Phasma sprung from artwork for Kylo Ren. Costume designer Michael Kaplan had pondered, "What if Kylo Ren were king of the stormtroopers, looking beautiful on the battlefield with flames reflected off his silver armor?" Although J.J. Abrams decided on a different approach for Ren, the artwork by Dermot Power stayed pinned to Kaplan's idea board, looking for a home. Kathleen Kennedy, in particular, was drawn to it, so when the opportunity came to create a new role of a stormtrooper leader, the silvery Ren idea was reforged as Captain Phasma's armor. It takes about forty-five minutes to dress Gwendoline Christie in the suit. "It certainly makes me stand up straight," Christie observed.

WESA GONNA GIVE YOUSA UNA BONGO

Technical Name:
Otoh Gunga Bongameken
Cooperative tri-bubble bngo

You Know it As:
Gungan submarine

Size Specs:
15 meters long

Performance:
Underwater speed of 85 kph

Weaponry:
None

Key Features:
- Flexible electromotive drive fins
- Corrugated construction for lightweight yet sturdy build
- Tri-bubble cockpit

Gungan technology has a sleek, organic look, as many of the frames that define their devices are *grown* rather than built. Their bongo submarines more resemble living mantas or squids than an unliving machine. This makes their crafts well suited for the watery depths but also may attract confused predators. The tri-bubble cockpit uses Gungan bubble-wort technology to project hydrostatic plasmatic shields, keeping the occupants dry but allowing them slow passage outside should escape become necessary.

A LITTLE BLUE LIE

For the film that would eventually be titled *Return of the Jedi*, Lucasfilm intended for some location shooting to be on public land in Arizona and California. To thwart an invasion of *Star Wars* fans and reporters—as well as to keep suppliers from overcharging the production—the fictitious working title *Blue Harvest* and the tagline "horror beyond imagination" was created. A fake logo for the movie was made, and it appeared on T-shirts and hats worn by the crew, who were told to say they were working on a horror movie.

RIDING ORBAK

There was a concerted effort to realize the orbak creatures entirely as practical constructions, but the difficulties of having to dress up a horse in makeup led to a hybrid approach. Beneath the costumed wooly coats of an orbak is a terrestrial horse. Their faces were designed to work as a mask worn by a horse, with the nostrils fitting where the horse's eyes are, and the orbak's eyes resting atop the horse's head. When the mask route was abandoned, the nostrils were shrunk in size. In the finished film, the orbak faces are computer-generated, tracked onto the horse's face by ILM artists. The orbaks were among J.J. Abrams's favorite effects in the film.

THE
DARK TIMES

With no intention to make more movies, Lucasfilm began drawing its attention away from *Star Wars* in the mid-1980s, with several long-running franchise initiatives drawing to a close. The newspaper strip of five years ended in March of 1984. The Marvel Comics series finished after 107 issues in May of 1986. The *Star Wars* Fan Club folded in 1987. The Kenner toyline attempted to stretch its series out with Ewoks and Droid figures, but these, too, fizzled out. As hard as it is to imagine in modern times, *Star Wars* was essentially dead during a period long-time fans have dubbed "the Dark Times."

THE LAST POKÉMON

The Last Jedi was in production during the initial craze of Pokémon Go, the augmented reality mobile game that populated the real world into a Pokémon hunting ground. More than a few cast and crew members were fixated on the game, as even Pinewood Studios could not keep the pocket monsters off the premises. During some down time, Kelly Marie Tran (Rose Tico) alerted Rian Johnson the presence of a Pikachu nearby. Johnson ran outside, only to discover that the crew had hand-drawn a Pikachu in chalk on the sidewalk as a lure.

A SITH DOUBLE-HEADER

Technical Name:
Not applicable; this is a
handcrafted item

You Know it As:
Darth Maul's double-
ended lightsaber

Size Spec:
49.5 centimeters (hilt-length);
4.40 centimeters (hilt-width)

When It Was Made:
During Darth Maul's
Sith training.

Key Features:
• Double blade "saberstaff"
configuration
• Control lock for
thrown attacks

An intimidating design that requires a true master of combat to wield safely and effectively, Darth Maul's double-bladed lightsaber is a dangerous Sith weapon. Its blades glow red from the corrupted kyber crystals contained within. Each end of the lightsaber can be ignited independently to function more like a traditional saber. But when both are active, Maul's reach extends, and his defensive prowess increases. Maul used this blade to kill Qui-Gon Jinn. The hilt, in turn, was sheared in two by Obi-Wan Kenobi.

A CAUSE FOR CELEBRATIONS

The return of new *Star Wars* movies that Episode I ushered in was a moment to commemorate for *Star Wars* fans, and Lucasfilm obliged by kicking off their first in what became a series of official conventions, Star Wars Celebration, in Denver, Colorado on April 30–May 2, 1999. More than 30,000 fans turned out, despite torrential rain! Since then, the show has moved around the world, including shows in Indianapolis, Los Angeles, London, Chiba, Orlando, Essen, Anaheim, and Chicago.

AN
EVIL BB

BB-8 was a breakout star of *The Force Awakens*, and *The Last Jedi* revealed his ball-shaped configuration was not a unique construction—there's a galaxy of BBs. For the Resistance flagship, additional BBs in different colors lurk in the background, but the most prominent new addition was BB-9E, a First Order unit with a gleaming black finish and a glowing red eye. Before he was named BB-9E (a moniker coined for merchandising purposes) the crew nicknamed the dark droid "BB-Hate."

ORIGINS OF THE FORCE

The Force is notably absent from some of the earliest versions of the *Star Wars* story. George Lucas drew some inspiration for Obi-Wan Kenobi and "the Force" after reading Carlos Castaneda's *Tales of Power*, an account of Don Juan, the Mexican-Indian sorcerer, and his experiences with what he calls "the life force."

THE *SOULLESS ONE*

Technical Name:
Feethan Ottraw Scalable
Assemblies Belbullab 22

You Know it As:
General Grievous's starfighter

Size Specs:
6.7 meters long; 5.4 meters wide

Performance:
Sublight speed of 90 MGLT;
atmospheric airspeed
of 1,100 kph

Weaponry:
• Two forward-facing triple laser
cannons

Key Features:
• Impervium hull coating
• Hyperdrive

This was General Grievous's spacebound chariot, when circumstances dictated he leave the bridge of one of his well-armed flagships. The systems aboard the compact fighter were optimized for the cyborg general's mechanical components, but his organic parts required a life-support suite aboard. Obi-Wan Kenobi absconded with the fighter after the Clone Wars. Its current whereabouts are unknown.

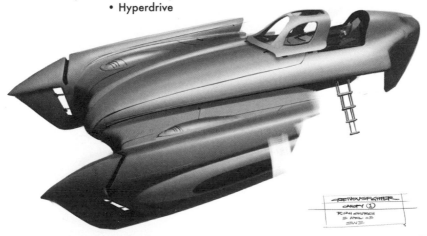

GRIEVOUS FIGHTER
CANOPY (1)
RYAN CHURCH
9 APRIL 03
SW3

REBEL
GRASSLANDS

Rather than be based out of an ever-mobile fleet, the Rebel Alliance had their headquarters on a grassland planet, Sice (city of Sicemon), in the rough draft for *Return of the Jedi*. Concept artists Ralph McQuarrie and Joe Johnston created striking vistas of windblown savannahs, punctuated by termite hill-like rocky formations. These concepts were later reused for the planet Lothal in the *Star Wars Rebels* animated series.

DUCKY D-O

The little wheelie droid named D-O started off as a castaway relic in Babu Frik's droid workshop in the early iterations of the story of *The Rise of Skywalker*. He was later transplanted to Ochi of Bestoon's ship (though he gets a much needed oil job at Babu's). D-O's nature of imprinting on BB-8 and following him about like a newly hatched duckling inspired his design, with his cone-shaped head evolving from the silhouette of a duckling's bill.

THE FAST AND THE FORCEFUL

Technical Name:
Kuat Systems Engineering Actis-class Eta-2

You Know it As:
Jedi Interceptor

Size Specs:
5.5 meters long; 4.3 meters wide

Performance:
Sublight speed of 120 MGLT; atmospheric airspeed of 1,500 kph

Weaponry:
• Two forward-facing laser cannons
• Two secondary ion cannons

Key Features:
• Separate hyperspace docking ring
• Extendable S-foil radiator wings
• Astromech socket

The last generation of Jedi fightercraft released before the end of the Clone Wars, the Jedi interceptor was a swift, compact, one-person vessel. Smaller even than the Delta-7 Jedi fighter, the Eta-2 has design cues that would hint at the future TIE starfighter program. The ship has extremely limited consumables, so it is designed for short-range missions, though the addition of a hyperspace ring extends its reach across light-years.

COMING TO A THEATER
NEAR YOU...

One of the starkest examples of how much the movie business and *Star Wars* itself has changed over the years is by looking at the number of movie theaters that carried each film on its premiere date. When the saga first started, seeing a movie on the big screen was the norm, and hit films could be expected to have a theatrical run of months, its growing audience as word of mouth spread. In the modern era, the industry heavily targets the opening weekend by debuting in as many screens as possible, clearing the way for the eventual home format releases that follow within the same year. Here are the theater counts for each film's debut.

Star Wars (May 25, 1977): 32

The Empire Strikes Back (May 21, 1980): 126

Return of the Jedi (May 25, 1983): 1,002

The Phantom Menace (May 19, 1999): 2,970

Attack of the Clones (May 16, 2002): 3,161

Revenge of the Sith (May 19, 2005): 3,661

The Force Awakens (Dec. 18, 2015): 4,134

The Last Jedi (Dec. 15, 2017): 4,232

The Rise of Skywalker (Dec. 20, 2019): 4,406

MUSICAL CAMEOS ABOUND

Episodes VII, VIII, and IX have numerous cameos from celebrity *Star Wars* fans, but *The Rise of Skywalker* had several musical-based ones worth noting. Piloting the *Tantive IV*, his face concealed behind a helmet, is Marcus Mumford, frontman of Mumford & Sons. Concealed behind the alien mask of a Resistance trooper named Engi Golba is Ed Sheeran.

LET THERE BE
LIGHTSABERS

For the first three movies, the lightsaber effect utilized rotoscoping: the artistic retouching of individual frames on a length of a film. For the first film, spinning wooden "blades" were coated with material that reflected the set's lights then photographed through a half-silvered mirror. Through the camera, the lightsabers appeared to glow, which was enhanced by rotoscoping. In the second trilogy, lightsabers were built with metal or carbon-fiber blades and were illuminated by CG effects in postproduction. For the latest three movies, CG continued to fill in the blades, but advancements in LEDs allowed for an illuminated prop that casts realistic glows and reflections on set.

THE THING
FROM ANOTHER
ICE WORLD

Renowned screenwriter and sci-fi/fantasy author Leigh Brackett joined George Lucas for early development of *The Empire Strikes Back* script. She had written screenplays for director Howard Hawks, including the classic 1951 sci-fi movie *The Thing from Another World*, which would be remade by John Carpenter as *The Thing* in 1982. Lucas cited the original film and the terror of a beast that had infiltrated an icy base during early creative meetings for *The Empire Strikes Back*.

A.K.A. REY

The Force Awakens' long journey from idea to finished film was filled with evolution, but one idea that remained constant from the start was that of a young woman's quest to become a Jedi Knight. In George Lucas's original outline, she was a 14-year-old girl named Taryn. In his subsequent iterations, she would briefly be named Thea and—believe it or not—Winkie. When writer/director J.J. Abrams came aboard, he simplified the names to placeholders. Kylo Ren was the Jedi Killer. Thea became Sally. Finn was called Harry. And the character that would be Poe was John Doe. As the film neared production, Sally became Kira (which stuck as a production code name), then Echo, and finally Rey.

WALK LOUDLY AND CARRY CLONES

Technical Name:
Rothana Heavy Engineering / Kuat Drive Yards All Terrain Tactical Enforcer

You Know it As:
AT-TE walker

Size Specs:
13.2 meters long, 5.7 meters tall

Performance:
Maximum speed of 60 kph on open terrain

Weaponry:
• Six anti-personnel laser cannon ball turrets (four front, two aft)
• One heavy projectile cannon

Key Features:
• Traction-field projectors on feet that allow for vertical climbs
• Low-to-ground construction for defense against enemy fire
• Flexible concertina mid-section for increased maneuverability

The combat armor of the Grand Army of Republic faced a baptism of fire, debuting in the first major engagement of the Clone Wars on Geonosis. The six-legged AT-TE acquitted itself well in its inaugural engagement, decimating incoming tank droid targets from long range. The AT-TEs were the backbone of many Republic armored assaults, and clone troopers grew to regard the thick-armored vehicle as a mobile haven from destruction.

COLONEL
KURTZWALKER

Although Luke Skywalker only barely appears in *The Force Awakens*, the concept artists had a lot to imagine based on the fragments of the story they were hearing as it developed. Rey was on a mission to seek out Luke Skywalker, who had disappeared. As described by George Lucas, Rey is like Willard going up river seeking out Colonel Kurtz, an allusion to *Apocalypse Now*. The story had Rey find Luke on a Jedi temple planet, but he is a recluse, withdrawn into a very dark space and needs to be drawn back from despair. Lucas approved one striking piece by Christian Alzmann that embodied this incarnation of Luke.

YOU SEEK TOYOTA, REDUX

Jodee Berry, a server working at a Hooters in Panama City, Florida, worked extra hard vying to see who could serve the most beer in a workplace competition with the grand prize being a "new Toyota." Led to the parking lot blindfolded, she was disappointed to find out she had, in fact, won a "toy Yoda," from Tiger Electronics. Berry sued her employer, alleging breach of contract and fraudulent misrepresentation.

POE DAMERON TIMELINE

Born on Yavin 4 to Rebel parents Shara Bey and Kes Dameron.

Age 6: Begins learning how to fly with mom in her A-wing fighter.

Age 8: Shara Bey dies, leaving Kes to raise Poe.

Age 16: Poe runs away from home and joins the Spice Runners of Kijimi.

Age 21: Poe returns home, abandoning the Spice Runners.

Age 25: Begins Academy training to fly with the New Republic.

Age 29: Defects from New Republic to join Princess Leia's Resistance movement

Age 32: Finds and recruits Kazuda Xiono to be a spy for the Resistance.

Age 32: Captured by Kylo Ren during the search for Luke Skywalker. Freed by FN-2187, a stormtrooper he names Finn.

Age 32: Demoted for insubordination during the Resistance escape from D'Qar.

Age 33: Promoted to general in the final push against the First Order.

DARK SIDE SNACKING

To accompany the hurrah of what was presumed to be the last *Star Wars* movie at the time, many brands partnered with *Revenge of the Sith* to translate the drama and spectacle of the rise of Darth Vader into snack foods. M&M's introduced, for the first time, *dark* chocolate centers to its popular candy brand. Pepsi rolled out its "Darth Dew" Slurpees at participating 7-Eleven stores, complete with Darth Vader cup-toppers. Kellogg's packed in light-up "Saberspoons" into its breakfasts cereals, and Frito-Lay dyed some of its Cheetos black ("Darth Vader Dark") and green ("Yoda Green"). For those who wanted to just imagine *Star Wars* as food without having to eat it, Hasbro released Darth Tater, a Darth Vader-themed Mr. Potato Head toy.

BOMBS AWAY!

Technical Name:
Slayn & Korpil MG-100
StarFortress SF-17

You Know it As:
Resistance bomber

Size Specs:
21.7 meters tall; 29.7 meters long;
15.3 meters wide

Weaponry:
- Three laser cannon turrets
- Six medium laser cannons
- Bomb rack

Key Features:
- Atmospheric containment field
- Detachable payload magazine

A dedicated bomber capable of hauling 1,048 bombs to a target site, the heavily armed craft can obliterate armored installations and capital ships with strategically dropped proton bombs. Artificial gravity generators within the bomber create the "drop" needed to release the bombs downward, assisted by magnetic field kickers that evens out the drop rate among the dozens and dozens of explosives.

UNMASKING
KYLO

As written, Kylo Ren was to have removed his mask earlier in the course of *The Force Awakens*, but as the edit came together, this moment was held until his face-to-face confrontation with Rey. This required digitally placing the mask onto Adam Driver's head in earlier scenes, a seamless effect pulled off by ILM.

ATTACK OF THE
BIGGER CLONES

It has now become standard for big blockbusters to get IMAX releases, complete with sequences specifically photographed with IMAX cameras. But back in 2002, IMAX was still mostly a format for special venue documentaries. Starting with *Apollo 13*, IMAX began using its proprietary DMR technology to upscale 35mm images to the IMAX format. *Star Wars*: Episode II *Attack of the Clones* was one of the first films to undergo this process for a limited IMAX release. It was a remarkable achievement given the resolution of the digital image was less than a 35mm film frame. Because of limitations of the physical film reel size at the time, feature films needed to be cut down to two hours or less to run as IMAX editions, which meant the IMAX release of *Attack of the Clones* is a unique cut never seen since.

ONE LAST DEJARIK MATCH
STAR WARS:
THE RISE OF SKYWALKER

EXT. LIGHTSPEED
The Falcon SPEEDS PAST CAMERA --

INT. FALCON - DAY
TIGHT ON CHEWIE, studying something. He leans down
and we BOOM DOWN to reveal the HOLOCHESS SET PIECES
in the f.g.. He's analyzing his next move.

Then we see the REVERSE: POE AND FINN, sitting close,
watching Chewie.

>   FINN
>   He can't beat us every time.

>   POE
>   -- and yet, he does.

>   FINN
>   How does he do it?

>   POE
>   That guy right there? I think he cheats.

Chewie TALKS: "Hey, I'm TRYING TO THINK HERE!"

>   POE
> I'm kidding! You're two-hundred and fifty years old!
>   Of course you're better than us!

```
                    FINN
    Take your turn already! You can't take forever,
                 that is cheating!

    Then there's a BEEPING -- annoyed, Chewie gets up and
    head off. Quietly, as the guys get up:

                    FINN
              I think he cheats.
                    POE
              Definitely cheats.
```

After a confused first foray into holochess in *Solo: A Star Wars Story* and a defeat by R2-D2 despite C-3PO's timeless advice to "let the Wookiee win," Chewbacca finally plays to win in *The Rise of Skywalker*, though the game does get interrupted. This brief scene was added during a stint of additional photography in July of 2019, and would feature animation from Tippett Studios to bring the stop-motion animation critters to holographic life.

A PRINCESS'S THANKS

Carrie Fisher passed away as Episode IX was in development. Director and co-writer J.J. Abrams faced the challenge of her absence head-on, realizing Leia could not be absent from a story that required her. By using previously unused footage from Episode VII, Abrams found a way to include her, something that Fisher cryptically seemed to predict in the dedication of her book, *The Princess Diarist*: "And special thanks to J.J. Abrams for putting up with me twice." Abrams said, "Now, I had never worked with her before *The Force Awakens* and I wasn't [originally] supposed to do this movie, so it was a classic Carrie thing to sort of write something like that and it could only mean one thing for me."

INDEX

20th Century Fox 5, 149

4-LOM 96

501st Legion 164

A Clockwork Orange 72

Abbey Road Studios 97

Abrams, J.J. 21, 34, 105, 112, 163, 175, 178, 193, 204

Acord, David 143

Ajan Kloss 171

Aki-Aki 156

Alderaan 31, 52, 74, 109, 158

American Graffiti 5, 166

American Zoetrope 23

Amidala, Padme 11, 52, 97, 98, 120, 124, 141

ANA 8

animatics 28, 106, 168

Apocalypse Now 195

Apollo 13 201

ARC-170 starfighter 33

AT-AT walker 76, 80, 116

AT-M6 walker 16

AT-TE walker 194

A-wing fighter 90

Baille, Kevin 106

Baker, Kenny 132, 138

Baker, Rick 68

Ballantine Books 77

BB-8 8, 142, 183

BB-9E 183

Beckett, Tobias 74

Berg, Jon 80, 163

Berry, Jodee 196

Biggar, Trisha 32, 161

Binks, Jar Jar 42, 66

Bjork 83

Black Park 171

Blue Harvest 177

Bocquet, Gavin 111

Bongo submarine 176

Boolio 150

Bossk 70, 96

Brackett, Leigh 9, 192

Bridge on the River Kwai 130

Burtt, Ben 6, 28, 30, 64, 93, 142

Butterbean 83

C-3PO 8, 149, 63, 83, 91, 96, 203

C-3PO's (Cereal) 49

Calrissian, Lando 7, 9, 12, 74

cantina 14, 68, 96

Canto Bight 122, 172–173

carbon-freezing chamber 74, 167

carbonite 74, 167

Cardington Air Sheds 69

Carida 74

Carpenter, John 192

Carter, Rick 105

Castaneda, Carlos 184

Chewbacca 12, 72, 74, 83, 152, 153, 160, 202–203

China 109

Chirpa, Chief 75

Christensen, Hayden 67, 115, 141, 161

Christie, Gwendoline 175

Classic Creatures 60

clone troopers 88, 92, 194

Clone Wars 19, 22, 27, 33, 37, 76, 81, 98, 102, 120, 157, 185, 188, 194

Close Encounters of the Third Kind 54

Cloud City 158

coaxium 167

Colbert, Stephen 42

Coleman, Rob 25, 143, 152

Corbould, Chris 119

Corellia 74

Corellian Engineering Corporation 7

Coruscant 87, 88, 98, 155

Coveney, Ivo 161

Cradle 2 the Grave 83

Crait 24, 71, 95, 129

Crumb, Salacious 60, 131

Cyu-bee, Weeteef 17

D-O 187

Dagobah 132, 145

Daley, Brian 162

Dameron, Poe 107, 135, 193, 197, 202–203

Daniels, Anthony 9, 49, 91, 162

Darklighter, Jake Lunt 114

Davis, Warwick 17, 51, 138

Day of Demand 52

Death Star 11, 22, 31, 33, 52, 98, 125, 158

Death Star II 21, 24, 33, 104, 147

Deluise, Dom 85

Dengar 96

Dern, Laura 107

destroyer droid 103

Diesel, Vin 83

digital cinema 55

Dozoretz, David 28

Dooku, Count 22, 98

Driver, Adam 18, 200

Ducsay, Bob 39

Dudge, Wolentic 17

Dudman, Nick 38

Dykstra, John 50

Dykstraflex 50

Echo Base 11

Eekway, Chi 88

Elom 131

Elstree Studios 26, 68, 109

Endor 21, 52, 75, 81, 104, 138, 155, 164

Ewok 6, 51, 75, 104, 138, 179

Ewokese 6

Exegol 11, 24, 59, 61, 127, 137, 153, 165

fathier 172–173
Ferrari 147
Ferrero of Germany 94
Fett, Boba 22, 70, 74, 136, 154
Fett, Jango 22, 70, 136
Feige, Kevin 121
Finn 27, 78, 122, 135, 153, 163, 172–173, 193, 197, 202–203
First Order 12, 18, 29, 37, 52, 69, 78, 90, 108, 116, 137, 165, 172–173, 183, 197
Fisher, Carrie 112, 204
Flash Gordon 5
Frito-Lay 198
Force, the 27, 39, 184
Ford, Harrison 23, 112
Fosselius, Ernie 30
Fox Studios Sydney 87, 92, 109
Freeborn, Stuart 68
From Star Wars to Jedi 60
Gasgano 85
Gathering, the 27
Gawley, Steve 133
Geonosis 22, 70, 76, 194
Geonosian 30
Geonosian arena 22
Geonosian droid factory 27, 141
Gilbert, Rose 105
Goodman, John 85
Grambling State University 164
Great Pit of Carkoon 40
Greedo 83
Grievous, General 27, 64, 185
starfighter 83
Gunga Din 130
Gungan 66, 120, 176
Gunray, Nute 120
Gurland, Robin 115
Guttenberg, Steve 83
Had Abbadon 59, 155
Hader, Bill 142
Hamill, Mark 36, 47, 112, 132, 162
Hardware Wars 30

Hasbro 118, 198
Hawks, Howard 192
Hickel, Hal 103
Hitchcock, Alfred 122
Holdo, Vice Admiral 107
Holman, Tomlinson 174
holochess 163, 202–203
Hoth 11, 52, 76, 145
Huttese 6
hyperdrive 33, 37, 90, 101, 108, 139, 157, 185
ILMxLAB 29
IMAX 201
Inch, Rob 10
Incom 33
Industrial Light & Magic 25, 42, 50, 62, 63, 67, 68, 83, 85, 89, 103, 109, 114, 127, 131, 133, 141, 143, 147, 152, 171, 178, 200
Italy 109
Jabba the Hutt 40, 43, 52, 60, 74, 131
Jackass: The Movie 83
Jackson, Peter 163
Jackson, Samuel L. 82, 110
Jakku 24, 57, 78, 119, 126, 153
Jawa 6
Jedi interceptor 37, 188
Jedi Knight 16, 27, 31, 98, 193
Jedi starfighter 157
Jinn, Qui-Gon 10, 31, 98, 124, 181
Johnson, Rian 39, 71, 107, 114, 122, 130, 135, 173, 180
Johnston, Joe 80, 117, 186
Jones, James Earl 72
Jordan 91, 156
Jukassa, Zett 88
Kamino 31, 136
Kaminoans 54
Kanata, Maz 27, 105
Kaplan, Michael 107, 175
Kasdan, Lawrence 170
Kashyyyk 109, 152

Kef Bir 21, 24
Kellogg's 49, 198
Kennedy, Kathleen 112, 173
Kenner Toys 118, 179
Kenobi, Obi-Wan 11, 27, 31, 43, 46, 65, 87, 94, 98, 124, 136, 145, 170, 181, 184, 185
Kershner, Irvin 47, 132
Kessel 74, 167
Ki-Adi-Mundi 82
Kijimi 19, 73, 190, 197
Kinder eggs 94
King, Perry 162
Kingma, Michael 152
Knights of Ren 48, 137, 156
Knoll, John 67
Knoxville, Johnny 83
Kryze, Duchess Satine 3
Kuat Drive Yards 76, 190
Kuat Entralla Drive Yards 116
Kuat Systems Engineering 70, 90, 157, 188
kyber crystal 27, 150, 188
Lai, Francis 9
Lane, Nathan 83
Lars Homestead 11, 34
Latifah, Queen 83
Lee, Christopher 83, 97
Legends of the Fall 13
Legislative Youth Program 12
Leibovitz, Annie 3
Letter Never Sent 13
Li, Jet 83
lightsaber 10, 21, 27, 42, 82, 83, 99, 150, 181, 193
Logan, Daniel 136
London Symphony Orchestra 9
Lothal 126, 183
Love Story 9
Lucas, Amanda 8
Lucas, George 5, 15, 20, 23, 34, 37, 41, 42, 44, 48, 54, 58, 62, 64, 66, 67, 72, 79, 82, 134, 140, 141, 144, 146

147, 152, 162, 164, 166, 168, 170, 174, 184, 192, 195

Lucas, Katie 88
Lucas, Jett 88
Lucasfilm 100, 125, 149, 163, 174, 179, 182
M&Ms 198
Madden, John 162
Mandalore 31
Mandalorian, The 60
Marvel Cinematic Universe 121
Marvel Comics 113, 179
Master Codebreaker 122
Maul, Darth 10, 31, 124, 181
Mayhew, Peter 152, 160
McCaig, Iain 32
McCallum, Rick 48, 111, 146
McDiarmid, Ian 38
McGregor, Ewan 67, 136
McQuarrie, Ralph 58, 59, 91, 117, 186
McVey, Tony 60
Mego Toys 118
Millennium Falcon 7, 74, 78, 93, 119, 153, 163, 202
Mimban 74
mirror cave 71
moisture vaporator 43
Mollo, John 96
Mon, Ephant 131
Morrison, Temuera 92
Mos Eisley 14, 68
Mos Espa 84–85, 146
Mozzer, Wizzich 17
MTV Movie Awards 83
Mumford, Marcus 190
Mumford and Sons 190
Mustafar 31, 61, 65, 98, 109, 159, 168
mynock 93
Naboo 31, 32, 56, 117, 120, 124, 164
Naboo starfighter 56

National Public Radio 162
Neeson, Liam 10
New Yorker 144
Nolte, Nick 23
Norway 151
Ochi of Bestoon 187
Odle, Hermi 131
Ohnaka, Hondo 27, 70
One of Us 71
orbak 69, 178
Order 66 102
Organa, Bail 52, 88
Organa, Breha 52
Organa, Leia 11, 31, 52, 74, 104, 120, 137, 138, 153, 197, 204
Otoh Gunga 176
Outer Rim Territories 22, 43, 65, 84, 95, 104, 145
Outlander Club 87
Oz, Frank 25, 36, 83, 132, 170
Papanoida, Baron 88
Paploo 138
Pagalies, Teemto 85
Palpatine 11, 38, 120, 125, 153
Panavision 48, 82
Pasaana 12, 156
Pesci, Joe 85
Pepsi 198
Peters, Brock 162
Peterson, Lorne 89, 147
Phasma, Captain 29, 57, 135, 175
Pikachu 180
Pinewood Studios 21, 119, 171, 180
Plutt, Unkar 78, 153
podracing 84–85, 98, 146
Poggle the Lesser 30
Pokemon Go 180
Polis Massa 11, 52, 120
porg 114
Porsche 100
Portman, Natalie 83, 115, 141
Power, Dermot 99, 175

Praetorian Guards 150
Prowse, David 72, 161
Q'ira 74
R2-D2 27, 45, 49, 83, 132, 138, 203
Raddus 52
Reagan, Ronald 169
Rebel Alliance 11, 19, 33, 74, 129, 186
Ree-Yees 130
Ren, Kylo 11, 18, 39, 61, 74, 95, 101, 108, 123, 137, 148, 150, 153, 175, 193, 197, 200
lightsaber 150
shuttle 101
TIE whisper 108
Resistance 11, 19, 52, 57, 90, 95, 129, 137, 153, 183, 190, 197, 199
Resistance bomber 199
Resistance ski speeder 129
Resistance Y-wing 19
Rey 11, 21, 27, 39, 71, 78, 95, 119, 123, 135, 137, 148, 153, 193, 195, 200
Ridley, Daisy 71, 123, 142
Roche Motors 129
Rogue One: A Star Wars Story 17, 69
Roose, Ark "Bumpy" 85
Rose, Tim 60
Rowling, Kyle 64
Royal Air Force 69
Russell, Kurt 23
sabacc 74
Sachs, Ann 162
sail barge 40, 60
San Diego Comic-Con 112
San Tekka, Lor 78, 150
Saturday Night Live 18
Scanlan, Neal 114, 156
Scarif 52
Schwartz, Ben 142
Shanghai Knights 83
Sheeran, Ed 190

Sice/Sicemon 117, 186

Sienar Fleet Systems 37

Sienar-Jaemus
Fleet Systems 101, 108, 139

Sidious, Darth 98, 165

Sing, Aurra 70

Sith 59, 61, 99, 181

Sith wayfinder 61, 165

Sith Eternal 11, 165

Skellig Michael 114

Skywalker, Anakin 22, 27, 31, 43,
44, 53, 65, 79, 85, 87, 97,
98, 115, 120, 124, 141

Skywalker, Luke 11, 14–15, 27,
31, 36, 40, 41, 43, 46–47, 52, 78, 82,
95, 98, 104, 120, 125, 132, 135, 137,
140, 145, 151, 153, 170, 195, 197

Skywalker, Shmi 98

Skywalker Ranch 115, 166

Slayn & Korpil 199

Smith, Kevin 112

Snoke 135, 137

snowspeeder 125

Solo: A Star Wars Story 17, 203

Solo, Ben 11, 52, 137, 150

Solo, Han 7, 23, 27, 52, 74,
137, 150, 153

Sony 55

Special Forces TIE 139

speeder bike 81, 138

Spice Runners 19, 197

Spielberg, Steven 20, 54, 168

St. Amand, Tom 80, 89

Star Tours 24, 127

Star Warriors 164

Star Wars Celebration 182

Star Wars Fan Club 179

Star Wars Rebels 126, 127, 186

Star Wars Resistance 18, 127

Star Wars: The Clone Wars 99, 127

Stewjon 31

Struzan, Drew 45

Su, Lama 83

Suotamo, Joonas 160

Switzerland 109

Tales of Power 184

Tarkin, Grand Moff 52

Tano, Ahsoka 98

Tater, Darth 198

Tatooine 11, 13, 14–15, 26, 31, 43,
84–85, 109, 117

Tattersall, David 111

tauntaun 27, 89

Tippett Studios 89, 163, 203

Taneel, Terr 88

Thailand 109

The Art of Star Wars 77

The Thing 192

The Thing from
Another World 192

Thomas, Roy 113

Three Outlaw Samurai 130

THX 174

THX 1138 125, 174

tibanna gas 167

Tico, Rose 122, 135, 172–173, 180

To Catch a Thief 122

TIE fighter 37, 139

TIE interceptor 90

TIE whisper 108

Tippett, Phil 89, 163

Tippett Studios 163, 203

Tournament of Roses 164

Toyota 149, 196

Trade Federation 103, 120, 125

Trade Federation battleship 103

Tran, Kelly Marie 180

Tudhope, Ryan 106

Tunisia 13, 91, 109, 146

Twelve O'Clock High 130

Tyerell, Ratts 85

Ugnaught 167

Undercover Boss 18

United Artists 5

United States Postal Service 45

University of
Southern California 166

Unknown Regions 165

Upsilon-class shuttle 101

Utapau 117, 168

V-wing fighter 37

Vader, Darth 11, 31, 46–47, 52, 53,
58, 61, 65, 72, 79, 98, 104,
128, 148, 161, 162, 198

Vanity Fair 34

Ventress, Asajj 99

Vietnam War 169

Walken, Christopher 23

Walpole, Peter 111

Wamoth 17

wampa ice creature 151

Warrick, Wicket W. 17, 51, 138

Watergate 169

Watto 83

Wazellman 17

We, Taun 83

Weazel 17

Williams, John 20, 53, 73, 97,
112, 128, 148

Willow 17

Windu, Mace 110

White Worms 74

Wodibin 17

Wollivan 17

Wood, Matthew 64, 142

X-wing fighter 11, 31

Yavin 4 69, 197

Yoda 11, 25, 36, 83, 132,
143, 168, 170, 196

York, Michael 85

Young Indiana
Jones Chronicles 11

Young, Duncan 6

Z-95 Headhunter 31

Zuckuss 94